Better Homes and Gardens®

Attics

YOUR GUIDE TO PLANNING AND REMODELING

Better Homes and Gardens® Books
Des Moines, Iowa

Better Homes and Gardens® Books
An imprint of Meredith® Books

Attics: Your Guide to Planning and Remodeling
Editor: Paula Marshall
Writer: John Riha
Designer: Michael Burns
Associate Art Director: Lynda Haupert
Copy Chief: Catherine Hamrick
Copy and Production Editor: Terri Fredrickson
Contributing Copy Editors: Carol Boker, Martin Miller
Contributing Proofreaders: Steve Hallam, Margaret Smith
Contributing Illustrators and Designers: Carson Ode, Mead Design, The Art Factory
Electronic Production Coordinator: Paula Forest
Editorial and Art Assistants: Kaye Chabot, Mary Lee Gavin, Karen Schirm
Production Director: Douglas Johnston
Production Manager: Pam Kvitne
Assistant Prepress Manager: Marjorie J. Schenkelberg

Meredith® Books
Editor in Chief: James D. Blume
Design Director: Matt Strelecki
Managing Editor: Gregory H. Kayko
Executive Editor, Shelter Books: Denise L. Caringer

Director, Sales & Marketing, Retail: Michael A. Peterson
Director, Sales & Marketing, Special Markets: Rita McMullen
Director, Sales & Marketing, Home & Garden Center Channel: Ray Wolf
Director, Operations: George A. Susral
Vice President, General Manager: Jamie L. Martin

Better Homes and Gardens® **Magazine**
Editor in Chief: Jean LemMon
Executive Building Editor: Joan McCloskey

Meredith Publishing Group
President, Publishing Group: Christopher Little
Vice President, Consumer Marketing & Development: Hal Oringer

Meredith Corporation
Chairman and Chief Executive Officer: William T. Kerr
Chairman of the Executive Committee: E. T. Meredith III

All of us at Better Homes and Gardens® Books are dedicated to providing you with information and ideas you need to enhance your home. We welcome your comments and suggestions about this book on attics. Write to us at: Better Homes and Gardens® Books, Do-It-Yourself Editorial Department, LN116, 1716 Locust St., Des Moines, IA 50309–3023.

Note to the Reader: Due to differing conditions, tools, and individual skills, Meredith Corporation assumes no responsibility for any damages, injuries suffered, or losses incurred as a result of following the information published in this book. Before beginning any project, review the instructions carefully, and if any doubts or questions remain, consult local experts or authorities. Because local codes and regulations vary greatly, always check with local authorities to ensure that your project complies with all applicable local codes and regulations. Always read and observe all of the safety precautions provided by any tool or equipment manufacturer, and follow all accepted safety procedures.

Contents

Evaluate Q&A

Encouraging answers to the most frequently asked questions about attic conversions.

Attics, renovated properly, provide light, bright, out-of-the-way spaces that offer a sense of privacy and separation from the home's main living areas. They're ideal locations for offices and guest rooms, or family rooms and playrooms. These are also romantic and intriguing spaces—no other room can quite match the appeal of living at the very top of a house. Open up an attic with a few well-placed windows or skylights, and you'll have access to daylight, air circulation, and great views. Sloped roof-lines create interesting interior spaces and are one of the unique benefits of establishing well-planned living space in an attic.

Structurally, most of the work is already done. Attics are framed and roofed, so converting an attic is a more cost-effective way to gain living area than building an addition. Exposed rafters and floor joists provide easy access for framing dormer windows, extending electrical circuits, locating heating and cooling ducts, and for adding insulation. Moving upward also is an especially good solution for small lots or where expanding outward may not be practical or allowed by local zoning ordinances.

Before you begin planning, you'll need to know if your attic meets certain basic building code requirements, if it can be accessed from the next lower level, and how much work is required for your ideal project. Finding answers to these and other frequently asked questions is the first step toward creating a great attic living area.

> *Off-white walls, quietly elegant furnishings, and a few well-placed skylights helped turn a 45-foot-long unused attic space into this serene and inviting guest suite. A crosswise seating grouping visually widens the long, narrow space.*

Won't my attic get too hot to be used for living space?

Because warm air naturally rises, an attic can become uncomfortably hot during summer months. In addition, attics don't usually have a great deal of circulation and allow hot, stuffy air to become trapped. However, if you're planning to turn an attic into living area, you can make upper-level spaces as comfortable as any room in your house.

You usually can extend existing heating and cooling systems to attic rooms. If controlling the temperature of the new space puts too much of a burden on your existing system, however, you can easily add supplemental heating and cooling to do the job. Filling wall and ceiling cavities with insulation reduces unwanted heat loss or gain, and adding windows and operable skylights encourages air circulation. For more information, see "Heating and Cooling Attic Spaces," pages 60-63.

▼ *This flat ceiling allowed easy installation of an extra measure of insulation to keep the temperature constant and comfortable. Spaces between the ceiling joists hold loose-fill cellulose, topped with a thick blanket of fiberglass batts.*

How do I know if I have enough headroom to turn my attic into a living area?

Most building codes require that more than 50 percent of the living area be at least 90 inches (7 feet, 6 inches) from the finished floor to the ceiling. This requirement ensures enough room to move about comfortably but allows for low spaces created by sloping roofs. These low areas generally make good locations for storage or furniture. When determining the ceiling height, take into account collar ties—the horizontal framing members used near the peak of the roof to tie together and strengthen roof rafters (see illustration, page 33). Codes consider the bottom of collar ties to be the allowable height.

In addition, any livable rooms must have at least 70 square feet and at least 7 feet in any horizontal direction. If you have a long room that is narrower than 7 feet, it won't meet code. And floor area that does not have a ceiling height of at least 90 inches does not count in determining the minimum number of allowable square feet. Side walls that intersect sloped ceilings do not necessarily have to define the allowable living area.

My attic is framed with trusses. What options do I have for converting it to living space?

Trusses, used to frame roofs, are composed of many diagonal framing members fastened together to create a web—a network of wood that results in great strength and stiffness with relatively light weight. Unfortunately, trusses will prevent you from converting your attic to a living area unless the entire roof is removed and replaced by conventional framing. That process is extremely expensive and time-consuming, and most likely not worth the costs.

Remember, do not alter trusses. Removing any of the web members will seriously weaken a truss system.

When building a new home, consider the future possibility of converting an attic to living space. This is an increasingly popular strategy, allowing you to plan for growing family needs but deferring the construction until a later date. Discuss your plans with an architect and builder—you'll want to make sure that your attic is framed with conventional rafters, not a truss system.

◄ Short side walls, called knee walls, often play an important role in the interior design of attic rooms. This space is usually high enough to allow different types of furnishings to be placed against a knee wall without having the pieces intrude on traffic areas.

Can I put a bathroom in an attic?

Yes, with careful planning. This means first evaluating the condition of attic floor joists and strengthening them if necessary. Strengthening joists is particularly important if you want to include a bathtub. Have an architect or building contractor evaluate your plans and inspect joists.

It is usually much easier to install a new bathroom near plumbing pipes and vent stacks already in place. This often means locating the new attic bath directly over another bath or the kitchen. If it isn't convenient to do this, you may have to use some imagination to gain access to drains, vents, and supply pipes. Solutions include concealing pipes in a downstairs closet or other out-of-the-way location, building a soffit in the room below, or building a raised floor in the attic and using the space to hide pipes. (Just make sure there's enough headroom for this last solution.)

It's a good idea to include a window in your bathroom for air circulation. If a window isn't feasible, consider a fan-assisted vent. For more information, see "Bathrooms," pages 68-71.

▲ *Although narrow, this attic bath has room for a vanity, sink, toilet, and bathtub. The unusual configuration of space created by a dormer window even permits a small vanity table and chair. Because the ceramic tile floor and the cast-iron tub are heavy, floor joists were strengthened.*

I don't have a stairway to my attic. Where can I get the space to put one in?

Finding the best location for stairs can become one of the trickiest problems to solve when planning attic rooms. Many houses don't include stairways to unfinished attic spaces—there's often a pull-down ladder or simply a covered access hole in a hallway ceiling.

Installing a new stairway means losing space on the floor below—borrowing square footage from a large room, such as a master bedroom, or sacrificing a hallway closet. Also, new stairs must comply with local building codes. Most codes require a maximum riser height of 7½ inches, a 9-inch minimum tread width, and at least 30 inches between handrails. This is a job that requires a design professional, such as an architect.

Another solution is building a stairway on the outside of your home. In certain situations, such as an attic office for an at-home professional who expects visits from clients, a separate exterior entrance is preferable. Before planning an outside stairway, check with your local building and zoning commission about any restrictions concerning exterior stairs. For more information, see "Finding Room for Stairs," pages 54-57.

Because of headroom considerations, the upper landing of the stairway often falls in the middle of the attic—where the headroom is greatest. Choose and place your furnishings to complement this "doorway." Older finished attics, such as this one, are usable even if their side walls are not tall enough to meet the height requirements for new construction.

Do I need to provide an "escape route" for attic rooms?

Establishing an alternative escape route for upstairs rooms is always a good idea. Building codes require emergency egress for any sleeping areas, including attic bedrooms. This is provided by an operable window with not less than 5.7 square feet of total surface area and located no higher than 44 inches above the floor. The minimum width of an egress window is 20 inches. Minimum height is 24 inches.

To allow a safe exit, purchase an emergency ladder. These are available at hardware stores or home improvement centers. Emergency ladders are designed to hook onto window frames and reach the ground below. They are made of flexible chain that can be folded or rolled for easy storage. An exterior stairway also provides an excellent emergency escape route. Before planning an outside stairway, check with your local building and zoning commission about any restrictions concerning exterior stairs. For more information, see "Finding Room for Stairs," pages 54-57.

Safety can be stylish. A generous egress window in the sleeping area complies with building codes and allows a quick, safe exit in the event of an emergency. It also provides plenty of light and fresh air.

My attic's roof rafters aren't very deep— They're only 2×8s. How will I provide adequate insulation?

Insulation requirements vary according to location and climate. You can estimate how much you need by using the chart on page 60 that equates insulation R-values with regional degree-heating days, or by calling your local building commission or Chamber of Commerce.

If necessary, you can increase the depth of existing rafters by adding a larger framing member alongside each one in a process called *sistering* the rafters. Remember, most building codes require a space above insulation for air circulation.

This space is important because sufficient air circulation prevents potentially damaging moisture and humidity from building up. For example, old rafters sistered with 2×12s have a nominal depth of about 11 inches—enough for 10 inches of insulation and a 1-inch gap leading to a vented roof ridge where moisture-laden air can escape (see "Insulating Attics," pages 61-63).

If you increase rafter size, be sure to calculate how much lower the finished ceiling will be to allow adequate headroom.

The homeowners liked the dramatic look of exposed rafters. To maintain the look and still have adequate insulation, they had the roof shingles removed, new joists installed on top of the roof sheathing, the spaces between the joists filled with insulation, and a new roof applied over the sheathing.

Should I have my roofing checked before proceeding with an attic project?

By all means, contact a roofing expert or general contractor to examine your roofing material and determine how many years of service it has left. If the roofing is old, cracked, deteriorated, or is missing shingles, it's a good idea to have it replaced to protect the investment you're about to make in your attic. You or a professional also should examine the inside of the attic roof. Stains on the underside of the roof sheathing, the rafters, or at the locations where vent stacks and chimneys pass through the roof may indicate a leak and be a warning sign that the roofing material is deteriorating.

A large percentage of the existing U.S housing stock is represented by houses built during the late 1960s and early 1970s. These houses typically feature roofs covered with asphalt shingles—a material that usually is guaranteed for 20 to 30 years—that may be due for replacement. In many cases, new roofing can be installed directly over the old. However, if your house already has more than two layers of roofing, it will need to be completely stripped before new material is applied.

New roofing protects valuable finishes and furnishings from possible damage due to leaks. It's good insurance against damage to new interior materials.

If the cost of roofing replacement isn't in your attic conversion budget, you may want to defer some aspects of your plan until you can pay for them. An example is to have the new space completely weathered-in with windows and insulation, but to put off installing drywall and trim until you catch up with family finances. The peace of mind you'll have with a new roof will be worth the wait.

Can I convert the attic space above my garage to living area?

Garage attics can make ideal locations for new living areas, provided they are not framed with trusses and meet the headroom requirements specified on page 7. Because there is no living area directly beneath a garage attic, they are especially quiet and private spaces that make ideal home offices or guest bedrooms.

Converting a garage attic is similar in most respects to converting an attic over living area. However, special attention should be given to the following:

■ A new stairway access must be integrated into the design of the project (see "Finding Room for Stairs," pages 54–57).

■ The floor joists generally are not intended to support the weight of a living area and must be strengthened (see "Floors," pages 38–41).

■ The living area should be insulated from the garage by installing fiberglass batts or other suitable material between the floor joists (see "Heating and Cooling Attic Spaces," pages 60–63).

■ The space must be heated by extending the existing system or installing a separate, thermostatically controlled system (see "Heating and Cooling Attic Spaces," pages 60–63).

■ Windows or dormers must be added to provide adequate daylight and air circulation (see "Windows," pages 46–49, and "Opening Up With Dormer Windows," pages 74–77).

▼ *A steeply pitched roof on this garage allows enough headroom for a private attic office.*

Using
Your Attic

Dream a little as you decide how best to use this versatile space

Each use of your attic has different requirements for preparation, accessibility, lighting, sound insulation, building codes, and many other elements. Think about how you want to use the space. Your family may have several different ideas in mind: perhaps a private home office, an extra bedroom, or simply a quiet place to relax and get away from the hubbub of household activities. Many attics are large enough to accommodate several options. Careful planning is key to getting the results you want. If your budget allows, consider hiring a design professional, such as an interior designer or an architect, to help you plan successfully.

Architecturally, attics can be unusual spaces. There may be sloped ceilings, nooks created by dormer windows, treetop views, and perhaps even a brick chimney. Any of these elements provide charming details of an attic room and help make your new space one of the most delightful areas of your home. Take advantage of an attic's special characteristics and add new ideas to increase your home's livability and value.

> *This attic room accommodates both a guest bedroom and a cozy home office. The two spaces are separated by an open framework of oak posts that defines the areas but doesn't block light.*

A Cozy Bedroom Retreat

Attics, quiet and out of the way, are perfect for bedrooms. Beds or low chests of drawers fit readily under the area's sloped roofs. For true convenience and luxury, include a closet and a bathroom.

Because getting to an attic requires climbing an extra flight of stairs, think about who will use an upper-level bedroom. As a master suite, or a child's bedroom, this shouldn't pose a problem. However, if the space is an in-law apartment, or for visiting relatives who are older, consider the occupant's ability to negotiate stairways on a regular basis.

Building codes require any sleeping area to include egress windows or doors in case of emergency. Egress windows must be at least 5.7 square feet and need to be easily accessible. Because attics are usually a considerable distance from the ground, provide an emergency ladder or stairway that allows

▶ *Gossamer fabrics, draped over the bed and table, and swirls of pastel paint on the walls and ceiling create a dreamy, in-the-clouds feeling perfect for an attic bedroom. Light, romantic furnishings complete the look.*

See Also:

Generous windows and an outdoor porch connect this bedroom to the great outdoors—and disguise the room's small size. Porch doors provide bedroom safety egress. The gable-end wall gets a little architectural intrigue with the high round window, perfect for stargazing.

access to the ground. Install smoke detectors outside each bedroom and over stairways. It's also wise to have a fire extinguisher handy. Make sure guests are aware of safety devices and how to use them.

Attics typically have a temperature zone different from other areas of the home. Because they're at the top of the house, they tend to be warmer. To maximize comfort, have the temperature-control systems for attic rooms isolated from the rest of the house and regulated by a separate thermostat (see "Heating and Cooling Attic Spaces," pages 60–63).

Also, including such useful amenities as telephone hookups, cable television lines, and a bathroom (see "Tucking in a Bathroom," page 18, and "Bathrooms," pages 68-71) truly will make this attic retreat a comfortable space.

Tucking in a
Bathroom

Putting a bathroom in a finished attic increases the convenience and livability of a rooftop suite. It also adds value to your home—a bathroom addition usually returns nearly 90 percent of your investment.

Meeting Code

Bathrooms have lower headroom requirements than other living areas—84 inches (7 feet) is adequate—so they can be configured to fit into small, odd-shaped spaces. A space 30 inches wide and 75 inches long—just 16 square feet—is adequate for a half-bath featuring a toilet and a sink. To include a shower or bathtub, you'll need a space about 5 feet wide and 7 feet long—only about 35 square feet. Tuck tubs under sloped rooflines, and build storage for linens and other necessities into low knee walls—the short wall created when side walls intersect sloping roofs.

Bathrooms need access to plumbing lines and vent stacks. The most convenient way to tap into a home's existing plumbing is to locate the new bathroom directly over an existing bathroom or kitchen.

Tub Techniques

Installing a tub often requires that you strengthen the floor framing so it can hold the extra weight. Also, cast-iron tubs are considerably heavier than models made of fiberglass or acrylic. Not only do cast-iron tubs require stronger floor joists, but they also can be difficult to carry up stairs. Be sure to consult with an architect or qualified building contractor who can advise you about the strength of your floor joists and whether stairways have adequate clearance for maneuvering a heavy tub to an attic location. You may have to purchase a smaller tub or install a shower instead.

See Also:

Bathrooms, pages 68–71
Floors, pages 38–41

◄ This beautiful bath was once a gable-end dormer window in a dusty, unused attic. Decked out in ceramic tiles, the bath is made only more charming by its vaulted ceiling. Locating this bath over an existing bathroom made plumbing hookups easier.

Attic Offices
That Work

A typical attic's perceived shortcomings become assets for a home office. Attics are quiet and located far away from household traffic—a prerequisite for getting work done. And limited floor space is not a problem. An 8×10-foot space is all that's needed for a desk, filing cabinets, and storage shelves. Local building codes typically require that new short side walls that intersect sloped roofs—knee walls—are at least 60 inches high. Office furniture puts these walls to good use: Built-in shelves, filing cabinets, and even desks fit neatly in such spaces.

Good lighting is essential. Generous amounts of daylight help ease eyestrain and prevent fatigue. However, you'll want to guard against too much direct sunlight or light sources that cause glare, especially important if your attic includes skylights. Be sure that skylights and other windows are equipped with fully operable shades that can block bright sunlight yet be opened on cloudy days or during morning and evening hours.

If you plan to have regular visits from clients, you may want to provide a separate entrance on the outside of your home. This should be clearly marked and easily accessible from the street. If possible, enclose this stairway and have it tastefully decorated to enhance its professional appearance.

Design a home office that works for your business. This small but efficient space includes two workstations—a desk for reading and doing paperwork, another for working at the computer. A swivel-based table between the two keeps supplies at hand. The quarter-round window in the gable end provides natural light and visual interest.

See Also:
Windows, pages 46–49
Insulating Against Noise, page 63

For long hours in your attic office, make it comfortable. Have temperature-control systems for attic rooms isolated from the rest of the house and regulated by a separate thermostat (see "Heating and Cooling Attic Spaces," pages 60–63). Consider insulating the floor with fiberglass batts to deaden sounds from rooms below (see "Insulating Against Noise." page 63).

A partition wall fitted with leaded-glass panels creates two distinct areas. It also allows plenty of natural light to reach both the home office and a sitting area.

Treasured Treetop Playrooms

Attics are intriguing and wonderful spaces for children. They'll appreciate having a room all to themselves; and if it includes angled rooflines and treetop views, so much the better. A child's attic playroom is a great place to consolidate toys, books, and games outside the household's main living areas.

One key to children's rooms is incorporating plenty of storage. Consider adding space-saving storage compartments and shelves along knee walls. You also can partition walls that divide attic spaces into bookshelves accessible from either side.

Carpet makes a great floor covering for children who love to play on their hands and knees. It also muffles the sound of busy feet. For added insulation from overhead noise, install fiberglass insulation between floor joists.

Keep safety a priority. Plan windows no less than 24 inches from the floor. If an existing window is less than 24 inches from the floor, try placing a piece of furniture in front of it to discourage youngsters from opening the window on their own. New stairways should conform to local building codes, and you should have existing stairways rebuilt if they don't meet code requirements. Add handrails to both sides of the stairway.

> Bright, cheery colors help turn an attic space into a child's dream room. Small-scaled furniture fits perfectly in the limited space. The window gets an extra measure of safety by placing a trunk in front of it. Wall-to-wall carpet helps muffle the sound of running feet.

See Also:

▲ This kid-pleasing attic playroom gets loads of character from walls painted to resemble log construction. A storage area built into the knee wall looks like a fireplace but is actually a shelf for toys. A cardboard cutout painted to look like flames keeps playthings stored out of sight.

Topflight Family Rooms

Equipped with a television, stereo equipment, bookshelves, and comfortable furniture, even a small attic family room can improve the livability of your home.

This is one of the easiest conversions—there is no need for plumbing, closets, or egress windows. Your main concerns are insulating the space, planning for light and ventilation with windows, skylights, and dormers, and selecting finishes for walls, floors, and ceilings.

Keep flexibility in mind. A family room should serve a variety of activities—reading, watching television, playing board games, or surfing the internet. Choose comfortable furniture that you can rearrange easily, and provide storage areas with doors for quick clean ups. Floor lamps, along with recessed

▶ *This simply furnished family room invites everyone upstairs for get-togethers with an adult-sized game table and a smaller table just for youngsters. A monochromatic paint scheme keeps the space bright and helps show off the homeowners' collection of fine antiques.*

See Also:

Walls and Floors, pages 34–41
Insulating Against Noise, page 63

▲ *With comfortable overstuffed furniture, this housetop family room is the perfect place for watching television, reading a book, or just sitting around and talking. Even small spaces become multipurpose: there's a game table in the window arch.*

fixtures and other ambient-light sources, keep the lighting scheme flexible. Be sure to include plenty of electrical outlets, two or three cable television outlets along the walls, and at least two phone jacks—one so that you won't have to scurry downstairs each time the phone rings, and another for a computer modem hook-up. For convenient access to snacks and drinks, add a small under-counter refrigerator. These units run off regular household electrical current and are easily moved if necessary.

Upper-Level Master Suite

Romantic and private, an attic master suite serves as a restful retreat at the end of the day.

A master suite goes beyond an ordinary bedroom. Its enticing amenities might include a bathroom, generous closet space with a changing room, and a sitting area. Extras could be a television, a stereo, an intercom, exercise equipment, or even a fireplace. Plan to take advantage of every square inch; you'll need at least 200 square feet of living space for even a modest master suite.

Investment Space

Creating a master suite is a good investment. A well-designed extra bedroom and bathroom can significantly increase the value of your home. For this reason, it may be worthwhile to consult an architect or other professional designer (see "Working with a Design Professional," page 81) so your suite is smartly integrated into the existing floor plan.

Because it is a room for sleeping, an egress window or door is required by codes. For true luxury, add a small deck, porch, or balcony (see "Adding an Outdoor Living Area," pages 64–67) to enjoy nature and satisfy egress requirements at the same time.

Safety and Systems

Be sure to have a safety ladder in an easily accessible spot in case you need to escape in an emergency. Include smoke detectors outside every door and one located over the stairwell. And, put a fire extinguisher in a handy location.

Attic locations tend to be warmer than other areas of your home. Make them completely comfortable by having the temperature-control systems for an attic suite isolated from the rest of the house and regulated by a separate thermostat (see "Heating and Cooling Attic Spaces," pages 60–63).

Rental Apartments

Apartments that provide rental income are considered separate living quarters from your home and must conform to local building and zoning regulations. Some local ordinances do not allow such apartments; other locales set strict guidelines for the size, number of bedrooms, maximum number of occupants, parking facilities, and fire protection measures. If you're thinking of turning your attic into a rental apartment, first check with your local building and zoning commissions, to make sure that your plans meet all legal requirements.

◄ *This spacious suite uses a partition wall with a gas fireplace to separate the sleeping area from a small living room. The partition wall also conceals the bathroom. Note how the chest of drawers is cleverly built into the knee wall to conserve space.*

See Also:

Bathrooms, pages 68–71
Storage, pages 72–73

Sunny
Getaway
Spaces

Sometimes dreams are loftier than time and budget allow. If you need to keep your plan down-to-earth, remember that an attic room doesn't have to be luxurious to increase you home's livability. Even a small sitting room, furnished with a few comfortable chairs and a lamp, is all that's needed to create a welcome retreat. Use the sitting room for reading, quiet conversation, working on a laptop computer, or playing a game. This also is a good use for a space that's too small for a bedroom or office.

To increase your options, include at least two electrical outlets, and consider a telephone jack and cable television hookup. Allow for at least one large window or a skylight for fresh air and daylight.

And, you don't have to finish the entire attic. Configure a sitting room at one end of a storage area and separate the spaces with a finished, insulated partition. Install an exterior-grade door.

▼ *Fitted with light and airy casual furniture, this 12×13-foot attic loft is one of the homeowners' favorite spots for relaxing. Positioned near an open stairwell, a skylight, and a generous window, the sitting area receives plenty of daylight.*

This door should be as wide as possible. A wide door-way and a stairway built to code will make retrieval of stored items easier and safer.

A simple sitting room also doesn't have to be completely separated from downstairs rooms. A loft features a low wall that overlooks living areas in the level below. To conform to building codes, this wall should be at least 36 inches high.

A skylight opposite a generous dormer window ensures plenty of natural light—not to mention headroom. This area is used regularly by the family for playing games and reading; the other end of this attic features a guest bedroom.

Elements of Style

Getting familiar with the basics of attic construction and design.

When converting an unused attic into living area, you need to select finish materials for walls, floors, and ceilings. Although these elements are some of the last items installed, making these decisions early helps ensure that your project proceeds smoothly and efficiently.

To make smart choices, familiarize yourself with the available options. Some elements, such as a tile floor for a bathroom, have specific requirements in terms of joist strength and subfloor thickness. Others have high price tags, making a major impact on your budget. Deciding on them at an early stage aids in developing a clear picture of the project's scope and total price. If you are working with a professional, such as an architect or interior designer, having definite ideas about the details of the finished space helps them anticipate potential problems, create solutions, and produce rooms that satisfy your needs.

Attics have a different construction and shape from other areas of your home. Understanding these underlying elements assists you in selecting materials that are in keeping with the unique properties of an attic space.

Keep a scrapbook of ideas. Cut pictures from magazines and collect product brochures. An idea scrapbook allows you to narrow your choices and convey your ideas to designers, builders, and others working on the project.

See Also:

◀ *A pair of beautiful windows provides plenty of daylight and lend visual appeal to this simple but appealing attic bedroom. The windows flank a chimney flue that has been covered with drywall and painted to match the walls. A collar tie, visible near the ceiling, is also sheathed in drywall and painted.*

Attic Construction

Attics generally have unusual shapes. To design this space effectively, it's a good idea to understand the basic construction techniques used to frame an attic and the necessary framing alterations to create comfortable living areas.

Attics are primarily triangular-shaped spaces created by gabled roofs. Variations of roof styles include hipped, gambrel, and mansard roofs.

No matter what roof style your house has, you can convert the attic into living space. Roofs that feature a steep pitch, however, are usually the best candidates because they offer the most headroom. According to building codes, at least 50 percent of the living area of a completed room must have at least 90 inches (7 foot 6 inches) from the finished floor to the ceiling. When evaluating an attic space for its potential, determining the amount of usable headroom is a primary consideration. No portion of a room that has a ceiling height of less than 5 feet can be considered living area.

Collar ties are horizontal framing members that span opposing rafters. Their purpose is to strengthen the roof system and prevent rafters from sagging. Collar ties are an integral part of your attic framing. Do not alter them without consulting an architect or registered structural engineer.

If the distance from the bottom of the collar tie to the finished floor is within code requirements for ceilings, then collar ties should not interfere with your remodeling plans. If they are lower than required, sometimes you can raise them. Consult an architect or registered engineer to see if—and how—you can move collar ties without jeopardizing the structural integrity of your roof system. Knee walls built under the rafters sometimes help strengthen the rafters, allowing the removal of collar ties. However, this arrangement may transfer the weight of the roof to the floor joists and require you to strengthen the joists. Again, consult a professional about using knee walls to support your roof system and removing collar ties.

Roof Styles

The shape of your roof goes a long way to determining how much usable space your attic will allow. Roof styles with many sloped surfaces, *such as the hipped roofs, offer less overall headroom than gable-end roofs on similar-size houses. The addition of dormer windows can add headroom.*

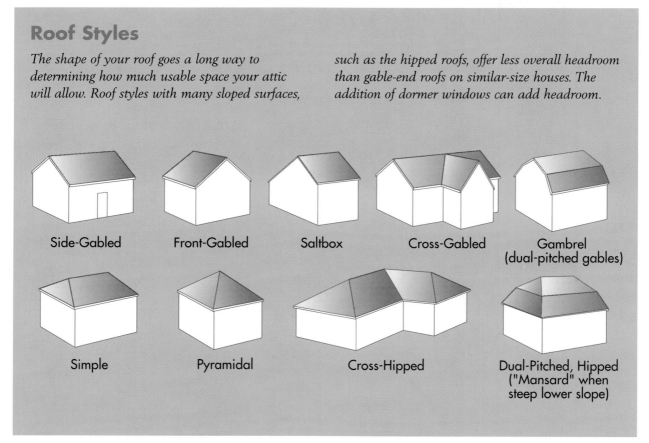

Side-Gabled   Front-Gabled   Saltbox   Cross-Gabled   Gambrel (dual-pitched gables)

Simple   Pyramidal   Cross-Hipped   Dual-Pitched, Hipped ("Mansard" when steep lower slope)

Typical attic room construction uses short side walls and a flat ceiling to form a more rectangular cross section than that presented by the triangular space of an unfinished attic. Vent empty space beneath the roof peak to prevent damage from condensation. Consider structural elements for the entire house, as shown in this diagram, when converting an attic to living space.

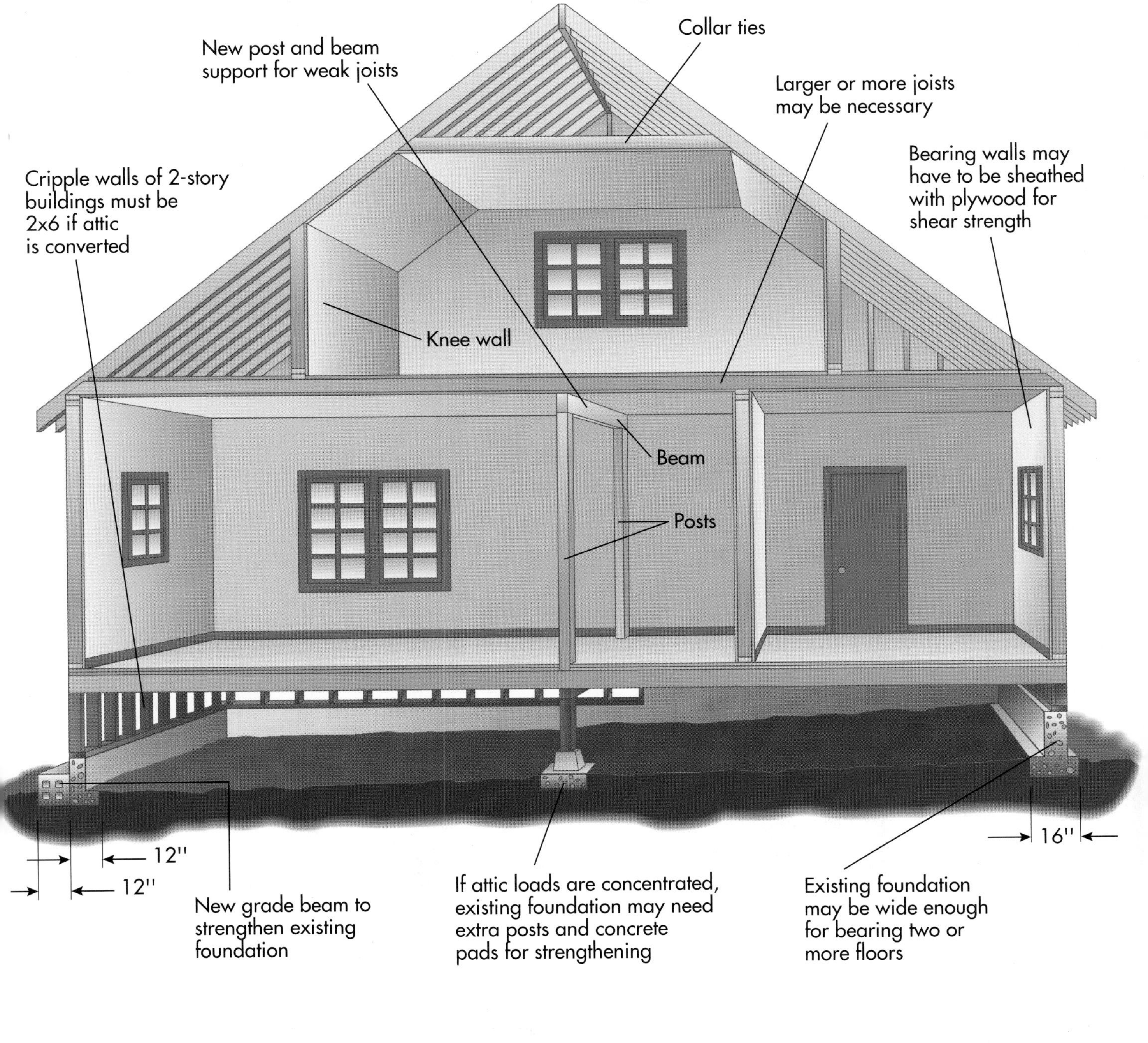

Collar ties

New post and beam support for weak joists

Larger or more joists may be necessary

Bearing walls may have to be sheathed with plywood for shear strength

Cripple walls of 2-story buildings must be 2x6 if attic is converted

Knee wall

Beam

Posts

12"

12"

16"

New grade beam to strengthen existing foundation

If attic loads are concentrated, existing foundation may need extra posts and concrete pads for strengthening

Existing foundation may be wide enough for bearing two or more floors

Walls

Your attic space likely has several different styles of walls. Peaked or triangular-shaped walls at the ends of the space are called *gable-end walls*. Low walls that extend between the floor and the sloped roofline are called *knee walls*. Walls dividing the space into different rooms are called *partition walls*. In addition, there can be dormer windows that create alcoves with yet another wall surface. All these different shapes and sizes (see illustration, page 33) create spaces that beg for imaginative design solutions. Are slanted areas considered part of the wall or the ceiling? Do finish treatments cover all surfaces or just some of the elements? By the very nature of their architectural lines, attics are whimsical spaces that lend themselves to your imagination and a variety of wall treatments.

Gable-end walls are also exterior walls. They are the tallest walls in an attic room and have a large influence on the interior design of the finished space. In an attic, they often serve as one of the few available vertical surfaces for hanging such typical decorative items as artwork. When converting an attic to living area, gable-end walls are good candidates for imaginative window configurations.

Knee walls help support rafters and define the sides of the interior spaces. According to building codes, areas with ceilings less than 7½ feet high cannot be counted as living space. Sometimes knees walls are used to define these boundaries.

▶ *Attics often don't have many vertical wall surfaces. Instead of constructing a partition wall, use free-standing folding screens to section off a room, create privacy, hang wall art, or serve as a decorative element. Existing low knee walls are livable because of the deep roof slope.*

To gain privacy in this attic bedroom, the designer turned what was once a railing at the top of the attic stairs into a solid partition wall and a convenient headboard for the bed. Windows inserted into the partition wall permit light from the skylight to permeate the interior of the room.

Simple freehand stripes painted on a solid background give texture and visually raise the ceiling in this stylish attic bath. Leaving the stripes off the slanted ceiling keeps the illusion of height. The sunny window, actually a trompe l'oeil painting, visually expands the space.

Knee walls are high enough for furniture, bookshelves, and fixtures such as bathtubs to be placed against them. These walls are often framed with 2×6 lumber to accommodate insulation (see "Heating and Cooling Attic Spaces," pages 60–63). For energy efficiency, cabinets, shelves, or cubbyholes built into the knee walls need full insulation.

▼ *Careful craftsmanship makes the wood-paneled wainscoting in this colorful bath fit neatly and pleasingly. Architectural elements, such as this alcove, often create awkward intersections between knee walls and sloped ceilings that can make installation of wainscoting difficult.*

Attic walls are typically covered with drywall and painted, wallpapered, or finished with wood. Placing partial partition walls in the space creates additional vertical surfaces for hanging pictures and other wall accessories. If your plans don't call for partition walls, adding a three-piece folding screen can provide space for displaying artwork.

An attic can have many architectural lines. When planning trim and moldings—even wallpaper borders—carefully consider how they will meet at your attic's many intersecting angles.

A trompe l'oeil fireplace visually warms up a children's room and adds an imaginative touch to this attic. And, it also takes up less floor space than the real thing.

A brick wall, left in place when an addition was constructed on the end of this house, was simply incorporated as an interesting element of this attic room. Cutting a doorway through the masonry allowed inclusion of the stairway in the addition, rather than having to reconfigure space in the existing house. The low knee wall wouldn't meet current code requirements but allows adequate headroom for the sitting area with the addition of a skylight.

Floors

Almost any flooring material works in an attic as long as the supporting joists are strong enough and in good condition. Some heavy flooring material, such as ceramic tile, requires additional layers of underlayment for stiffness. Also, building codes dictate the size of floor joists based on the intended use of your attic space and the kinds of furnishings planned. To ensure your joists will support the additional weight of flooring material, have an architect or structural engineer evaluate their condition.

You must install a subfloor before you apply finish flooring material. This is usually a layer of ⅝-inch-thick plywood or particleboard rated for this use. A subfloor provides a smooth base and stiffens the floor system. While the installation of the subfloor is not difficult, getting bulky sheets of 4×8-foot material into the attic presents a problem. Be sure to discuss with your contractor how to get these large materials into the attic. In some cases, access may be gained only by cutting away part of a gable-end wall. This process—and the repair of exterior walls to your satisfaction—should be specified in your contract (see "Working With A Contractor," pages 110–111).

You should plan the entire project before subflooring is put down so that you can install any wiring, ductwork, plumbing, or sound insulation between the joists before they are covered.

Carpet

Carpet is an excellent covering for attic floors. The look of carpet is warm and inviting, and it is available in a variety of colors and textures. Carpet installs easily and is a cost-effective choice. Depending on the grade of carpet you select, plan to spend between $12 and $30 per square yard for carpet, installed. Combined with a good-quality pad, carpet is effective at muffling sounds—an important consideration if attic rooms are located over bedrooms (see "Insulating Against Noise," page 63).

Wood Flooring

Wood flooring is another good choice for attic rooms. It is beautiful, durable, and complements a variety of interior design schemes. It is also a hard surface that offers little insulation against unwanted noise and may amplify footfalls. To help muffle sounds, use rugs in high-traffic areas. Typical wood flooring, such as oak or maple strip, costs about $6 to $8 per square foot, installed.

Paint

Paint offers a low-cost alternative that you can apply directly to a subfloor, providing it is smooth, free of defects, and all nail or screw heads are flush or driven below the surrounding surfaces. For best results, fill nail holes and sand smooth. Decorative paint techniques, such as checkerboarding or stenciling, are especially fun do-it-yourself projects. Use a good-quality latex paint and finish the job with two coats of polyurethane for protection against scuffs and scrapes. Muffle footfalls with rugs placed in high-traffic areas.

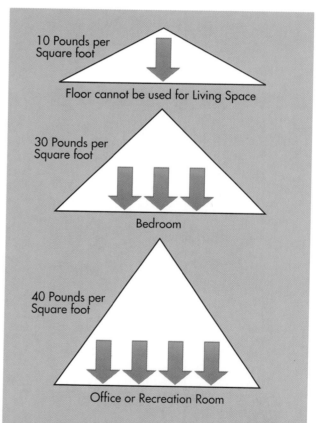

The strength of the floor joists will determine the use you can make of your attic space. If pressure estimated at 10 pounds per square foot causes joists to sag or "deflect," they must be strengthened before you can use the area as living space. Always have an architect or licensed structural engineer make these estimates.

▲ *An ordinary wood strip floor is given new life with paint. The large checkerboard pattern is well-scaled to the size of the room and features a hand-painted, decorative border.*

Ceramic Tile

Durable, beautiful, and available in many styles, colors, and textures, ceramic tile is rarely used as a general floor covering in an attic. But it is a good choice for bathrooms where you also can use it for walls and tub or shower enclosures. Its weight requires an extra layer of subflooring to ensure stability. Have an architect or structural engineer evaluate the strength of the floor joists before choosing ceramic tile. Although installation is straightforward, it is a relatively slow process. Expect to pay between $5 and $15 per square foot for a professional to install medium-grade ceramic tile on your attic floor.

Ceramic tile is waterproof and especially durable— a good choice for bathroom floors. Gleaming white floors featuring 6-inch square tile combine with tile walls to give this bathroom a classic finish.

Laminate Flooring

Plastic-laminate plank flooring made from the same material used to make laminate kitchen countertops, is extremely durable. It resists stains, abrasions, and moisture. The planks usually imitate the look of wood and provide an attractive option for playrooms, offices, and family rooms. Because the material sits on a cushioned backing, laminate-plank flooring offers some sound insulation, but you'll want to add area rugs to control noise. The installed price of a laminate plank floor runs between $7 and $9 per square foot.

Vinyl

Vinyl sheet goods and vinyl tiles are tough, cost-effective floor coverings for any room. You'll find a variety of styles, colors, and patterns to match most interior design schemes. For any vinyl product, make sure the subfloor is smooth and free of defects prior to installation. Otherwise, imperfections, such as cracks, eventually will show through the flooring and can even cause the material to tear. Repair cracks and other defects in the subfloor with filler and sand absolutely smooth.

Carpet makes rooms feel cozy and is a good choice for bedroom floors. It also helps muffle footfalls and insulates against noise from below.

▼ *Vinyl floors can be stylish and colorful. This floor features two different colors of vinyl cut into large squares that are arranged into a checkerboard pattern. The result is subtle and elegant.*

Ceilings

Attic ceilings typically slant inward, giving these spaces their unique character. A variety of unusual elements, such as exposed collar ties and dormer window alcoves, may accompany ceilings. Keep this in mind when planning the use and look of the finished space.

Rafters

Occasionally, roof rafters need strengthening before converting attics into living spaces. Rafter sizes are calculated to support the weight of the roof and any snow loads that might accumulate during winter. However, the additional weight of finish materials, such as drywall, may require stronger rafters. Also, the width of the existing rafters may not provide enough room for adequate insulation. The amount of insulation needed varies with the climate, but in most colder regions, attic insulation rated at R-38 is recommended. That's more than 12 inches of fiberglass batt insulation. And, it's very important to allow at least a 1-inch gap above the batts (see illustration, page 62) so that air circulates and excess moisture vents to the outside (see "Heating and Cooling Attic Spaces," page 60–63). All these factors may mean that the roof structure needs more rafters, or enlargement of existing the rafters, for strength. Consult with an architect and a reliable heating and cooling contractor to discuss the structural alterations to your home.

Headroom and Finishes

Most building codes require that more than 50 percent of the living area has headroom of at least 90 inches from the finished floor to the ceiling. Consider creating a flat ceiling rather than a peaked one (see illustration B, page 44). A flat ceiling provides an area for such fixtures as recessed lights and ceiling fans. In addition, the empty space above a flat ceiling can serve as a good place for running ductwork or wiring and acts as a component of the ventilation system, making the installation of a roof vent unnecessary.

The structural
members of this
barn-like space were
left exposed to allow
the room to have a
rustic look. Comfort
was accounted for,
however, by adding
insulation to the
outside of the roof,
then covering the
insulation with
roofing material.

When you finish attic ceilings, first decide whether the slanted walls are part of the wall or part of the ceiling. Some design schemes call for all surfaces to use similar finish material or color of paint; others prefer that each surface differs from the next. Still others try to present unique treatments designed especially for slanted attic ceilings. If you are working with design professionals, ask them to prepare perspective color drawings that depict the finished scheme so you can evaluate them before coming to a decision.

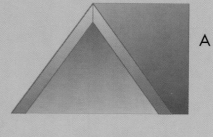

➤ This unique decorative treatment features a series of large black-and-white prints placed in a dark wood frame screwed directly to the slanted area. The display is a single unit, securely attached to this gravity-defying position.

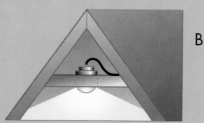

▲ This beadboard ceiling is beautiful, but such treatments pose logistical problems for cutting and fitting trim around the many odd angles formed at the intersections of walls, sloping ceilings, dormer windows, or knee walls. Do a scale drawing and do the math first to make sure your idea is feasible.

A

B

Finishing an attic ceiling to its peak (A) creates an interesting architectural space, but installing even a small portion of flat ceiling (B) permits the installation of recessed lighting and leaves room for both running wires and ductwork.

The collar ties for this attic space sit high enough in the unusually tall ceiling to be unobtrusive, and they add an element of architectural interest. To keep this soaring space from becoming a dark spot, the designer added lights between each pair of collar ties.

Windows

Unfinished attics rarely let in enough daylight and ventilation for living areas, necessitating the installation of windows or skylights as part of the conversion plan. Locate windows or skylights at opposite ends of the room for cross-ventilation and to take advantage of natural light all day.

Windows typically are installed in vertical wall surfaces, such as the ends of gable roofs. Skylights—sometimes called roof windows—are installed on sloped roofs. Another way to open up attic rooms is by adding dormer windows (see pages 74–77.)

Use any shape or size window, as long as it meets code requirements and does not weaken the structural integrity of the end walls. Codes typically require the square footage of windows total at least one-twentieth of a room's floor area. When you are choosing windows for end walls, keep these points in mind:

■ If possible, keep the major portion of a window at eye level. Windows that are too low to see the horizon create uncomfortable viewing angles. Windows placed higher than eye level are fine—they'll gather interesting views of the sky. Take privacy into consideration—if you can see your neighbors, they can see you.

■ Avoid windows low enough for young children to run into. For safety purposes, keep windowsills at least 24 inches above the floor.

■ Consider the placement of furniture in your attic rooms before adding windows. You don't want to end up putting a tall chest of drawers or other large piece of furniture in front of a window or reading chairs across the room and away from the light.

■ Look at window placements from the outside, too. They should be in harmony with your home's architecture. If your house is in a historic district, you should check with your local building or historic commission. Strict rules or codes may govern changes to the exterior of your home.

Installing skylights efficiently adds daylight, allows fresh air to circulate through attic rooms, and maintains privacy. Placed over a bed, a skylight allows views of stars at night. Skylights come in many different styles and with a variety of options to fit your needs. Make sure your skylights have insulated, tempered glazing for energy efficiency

A triangular grid of windows fills the gable end of this attic space and emphasizes the upswept angles of the roofline. Several lower panes are operable, allowing air circulation during warm weather. If you have a snug attic space like this, talk to a contractor about possible ways to adapt your ideas to meet building codes.

and safety. When planning for skylights, consider these possibilities:

■ Fixed skylights cannot be opened but are usually the most economical units. Install fixed skylights over stairwells or hallways to increase available daylight and to ensure safety, or pair them with skylights that open to help keep costs down.

■ Fixed, vented skylights include a small vent that opens and closes to allow air to circulate. These types of units are less expensive than skylights that open fully.

■ Vented skylights open with a hand crank, control rods, or electronic controls. Vented skylights allow fresh air to circulate through attic rooms. Make sure your vented skylight is equipped with an insect screen to keep out pests.

■ Egress roof windows comply with code requirements for bedrooms and can provide safe exit in case of an emergency. The

▼ *Skylights are ideal for attic bathrooms because they admit lots of daylight while preserving privacy. Skylights that open encourage air circulation and can help reduce the amount of moisture typical in bathrooms.*

bottom edge of code-compliant egress windows must be located no more than 44 inches from the floor, and the moveable portion of the window must open to at least a 45-degree angle.

Because skylights face upward, solar heat gain—the warming effect caused by sunlight entering your home—can be uncomfortably high. The best way to prevent unwanted solar gain is to equip skylights with movable shades or blinds. That way, you control the amount of sunshine entering attic rooms.

When planning for skylights, it's a good idea to understand the position of your house and roof compared to the sun—the orientation—at different times during the year. Each orientation has unique characteristics.

■ South-facing skylights are excellent in winter, but they are sure to gather lots of sunlight during the rest of the year, too. Equip them with light-blocking shades or blinds. South-facing skylights work best in cold climates.

■ East-facing skylights gather morning sun but have less solar gain as the day progresses and becomes hotter. East-facing skylights are appropriate for all climates.

■ West-facing skylights gather direct late afternoon and evening sun and can lead to extreme solar heat gain in warm climates. West-facing skylights are generally not recommended.

■ North-facing skylights gather the least amount of direct sunlight during winter months. However, they provide excellent general ambient light, sometimes called *painter's light*. Because north-facing skylights gather solar heat gain during summer, when the sun is directly overhead, you may want to equip them with movable shades or blinds. Light-diffusing shades—ones that are light-colored or translucent—help create the appealing ambient painter's light even in summer.

▶ *A customdesigned box bay window was an essential element of an attic conversion in this 100-year-old cottage. The window, nearly 8 feet tall, is itself a small addition, with its own roof and siding. Inside, the window sits in a recess that jazzes up the room's design.*

▲ *A new double-hung window helped open up the attic of this 1920s bungalow for a bedroom conversion project. By installing an arched transom over the double-hung unit, the new window echoes the arched front entryway and establishes architectural harmony.*

Understanding Color

Creating the right color scheme often requires some experimentation. This is especially true in attics. Sloped ceilings, short walls, and a surfeit of strong, shifting light create a variety of textures and shapes that seem to change with each new season—and even over the course of a day. A reliable method for selecting a color scheme is to keep trim and ceiling colors neutral, and use impact colors only on large fields, such as walls. That way, if you change your mind, you won't have to redo the

Neutral and off-white colors provide a good all-around background and help reflect ambient light, keeping attics bright and upbeat. They also offer uncompetitive backgrounds for antiques and for furnishings featuring muted fabric hues.

entire space—just the walls. Fortunately, repainting walls is relatively easy.

It's no secret that colors affect mood. While color preference is certainly subjective, the colors you select for your attic rooms play a major role in determining how the rooms feel to most people. Here's a quick primer on understanding how color influences attitude to help you create the right mood for your attic.

▷ Muted greens are perfect for your bedrooms and other restful environments. However, even in rooms that are painted the most peaceful of greens, don't expect kids to stay quiet for very long!

Active Colors

Active colors, such as yellow, red, and orange, are bright and warm. They are associated with high energy and playfulness, which explains why children often find them especially attractive. These colors are good for playrooms, offices, and game rooms—areas that are intended for alert, upbeat activities.

▲ The basic tone of this attic space is crisp white, but just a touch of blue makes the whole space feel livelier. Although blue is classified as a passive tone, here it actually helps to create an energetic color scheme.

Passive Colors

Passive colors include cool greens, blues, and purples. These are calming, pacifying hues that encourage rest, relaxation, and quiet contemplation. These colors work well in bedrooms, reading areas, and sitting rooms. They are just as effective when used as accent colors against white or neutral walls.

Neutral Colors

Neutral colors are background colors you can use to create transitions between rooms or fields of different color. They include shades of brown, beige, gray, and white. They are usually not associated with specific moods, although darker shades of brown tend to work as passive colors. Neutral colors on walls help emphasize furnishings and accent colors. A prized collection of fine antiques or colorful cottage furniture shows up well against a neutral background.

Making Attics Livable

Addressing the special needs of attic rooms

Attic spaces are similar in many respects to other areas of the home, but certain aspects require special consideration—heating and cooling the space, for example, lighting rooms with high or low ceilings and angled walls, and, if necessary, adding stairs.

Make a List

Start by listing your objectives for your attic conversion. Prioritize your needs by creating two lists. The primary list starts with the critical attributes, such as the intended use of the space—a spare bedroom for guests or a place for the kids to watch television. Add the elements that are essential. For example, your attic office needs absolute privacy and quiet, or the attic family room must include lots of storage.

The second list is a "wish list" of your favorite ideas—a large round window overlooking the garden or an attic bathroom. As you discuss your plans with a designer or building contractor, get rough cost estimates for items on your wish list. You may not include them all, but having a wish list will help you prioritize your options when it comes to final plans and budget.

Know the Code

Become familiar with local building codes and the various restrictions and requirements that help make attic rooms safe. Consult an architect, interior designer, or qualified building professional to help you make informed decisions and to make you aware of building codes as you make choices (see "Working With a Design Professional," page 81).

◀ *An empty attic space is like a blank canvas. With a little creativity, you can have a masterpiece. This spacious, comfortable bedroom was an unfinished attic. The homeowners added a dormer, built in two armoire-style closets with a window seat, and put a ceiling under the collar ties. Sunlight, fresh air, and space are maximized, and the electrical, heating, and cooling systems are concealed.*

Finding Room for Stairs

Building a stairway to access attic rooms becomes one of the most difficult problems for an attic conversion. Most attics are accessed only by two unsuitable means: by a hatch located in a hallway or closet, or by a pull-down ladder. (Pull-down ladders cannot legally be used as stairways to finished attic rooms.) Some older homes have stairs to the attic, but they are often too narrow and/or steep for regular use. Rebuilding is required.

Stairs take up a considerable amount of space—space that isn't readily available in many existing houses. Most likely, you'll need to "borrow" space from a bedroom, hallway, or closet on the level directly below. Sacrificing an entire room downstairs to gain overall living space in new attic rooms is an option, but consider fully how that will affect the main living area. Wherever the space is drawn from, make sure the stairway is convenient; avoid locating it where passing through another room is necessary.

Finding the needed floor space is only part of the solution. Adequate headroom is also a concern. Because of sloped roofs, the stairway often must enter the attic at or near the middle, where headroom is sufficient. Other building code requirements stipulate minimums for width and steepness, and require that the entire run of stairs have at least 84 inches of headroom when measured vertically from the front edge of any step. To make sure all the criteria are met, seek the advice of an architect or other qualified design professional (see "Mapping the Changes," pages 82–89, for plans that include solutions for stairways).

> *If you're building a new stairway, there's no need to be shy about design. The owner of this turn-of-the-century house added stepped shelves to show off these handmade lamps, then echoed the design with stepped wall cutouts to display pottery.*

▶ *An exposed staircase to an attic retreat is an airy, integral element of this home's interior design. The corner made by the stairs' turn created space for an intimate table for two. An angled support under the landing allows an open passageway.*

If adding stairs to your attic presents a challenge, think creatively. There are a number of configurations and solutions to choose from.

Straight Stairs

Straight stairs are the easiest to build, but the long, straight area required for their installation is not often available. A standard 3-foot-wide straight stairway that rises about 8 vertical feet needs at least 12 horizontal feet of run and 3×3-foot landings at each end.

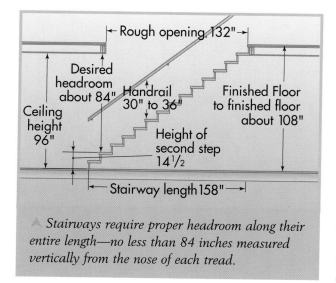

Stairways require proper headroom along their entire length—no less than 84 inches measured vertically from the nose of each tread.

L- or U-shaped Stairs

Stairs built in an L- or U-shape adapt better than straight stairs to limited available space. Most often, the upper portion of the stairway is built to follow the roofline. This conserves interior space by allowing the stairs to be positioned close to an outside

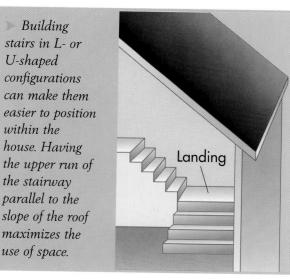

Building stairs in L- or U-shaped configurations can make them easier to position within the house. Having the upper run of the stairway parallel to the slope of the roof maximizes the use of space.

wall. It also allows you to terminate the stairway near the middle of the attic where headroom is adequate. Stairs configured in an L- or U-shape stairs usually require a landing at every right-angle turn. Because landings are usually a minimum of 3×3 foot, L- and U-shaped stairs take up more total area than straight stairs.

Dormers

Adding a dormer with a window may be the best way to accommodate stairs that are particularly difficult to configure or fit into the available space (see "Opening Up Attics With Dormer Windows," pages 74–77). A dormer provides the necessary headroom required at landings or at the location where the stairs enter the attic. Adding a dormer to accommodate a stairway significantly increases the expense of doing an attic conversion. But the compensation in ease of accessibility and the gain in daylight and ventilation may make it worth the price.

A dormer window added over a landing creates the headroom necessary for a code-compliant stairway. A dormer also illuminates the stairway with natural light.

Spiral Stairs

Spiral stairs take up much less floor space than conventional stairs and add an architecturally interesting element. Their diameters vary from 4 to 6 feet. Local building codes typically specify that a spiral stairway cannot serve as the primary access to an attic room if the total usable living area of the attic is more than 400 square feet. Spiral stairways are difficult for some people to climb, and moving large objects, such as furniture, up or down spiral stairways presents quite a challenge.

Stairway Tower Addition

Adding on to your house to provide stairway access to the attic is an expensive solution requiring a new foundation, roofing, siding, and insulation. As part of a major remodeling, however, the cost may be justified, especially if this is the best solution for attic access. If you want access to the attic directly from the outside, for an apartment or a home office, this is the perfect solution.

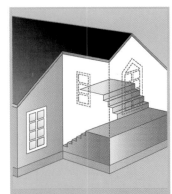

▲ *A stairway tower addition offers a good solution to accessing attic spaces. Have it designed to remain in keeping with the style of your home.*

▼ *This attic-based home business features two stairways—the homeowner enters from a stairway inside the house, and clients enter from an outside stairway.*

▲ *Spiral stairs offer space-saving access to attic rooms. Many spiral stair units come pre-fabricated and readily install in less than a day. They are architecturally interesting but may be difficult for older people or very young children to negotiate.*

Creating Good Lighting

The options for bringing daylight to attic rooms are in no short supply. Windows, skylights, and dormers can all help provide plenty of daylight for attics. And, attics often are positioned above daylight-blocking obstructions, such as neighboring buildings and lower branches of trees. Adding artificial lighting, however, requires well-thought-out solutions. Sloped rooflines create awkward locations for some traditional fixtures, such as recessed ceiling lights or wall sconces. Deciding how to add artificial lighting will help you create comfortable, livable, and safe attic rooms. As you plan, be sure your lighting scheme conforms to building codes by providing a light that is operated by a wall switch installed at the entry to each room. For a single attic room, the entry is considered the top of the stair access.

Consider lighting when deciding on the configuration of your ceiling. If you are thinking of finishing your ceiling to a peak, you may want to add a small section of flat, horizontal ceiling area to provide space for recessed fixtures or even a ceiling fan (see "Ceiling Fans," opposite). Make sure the ceiling

▼ *This cozy bedroom features several sources of light—a large window and three skylights for daylight, a row of adjustable track lights to help create both ambient and task lighting, and a pair of table lamps for night-time reading.*

height is adequate. Most building codes require that more than 50 percent of the living area has at least 90 inches from the finished floor to the ceiling.

Be sure that your lighting plan includes two types of light: Ambient light is soft, non-directional, diffuse lighting typically created by reflecting light off a surface, such as a ceiling. Task lighting is a bright light directed at a specific area to assist you in accomplishing particular goals, such as reading or working at a desk or hobby table.

An attic's unconventional shape will present a challenge in creating ambient light. Collar ties—the horizontal framing members used to stiffen roof rafters (see illustration, page 33)—can camouflage sources of indirect lighting. Install incandescent or fluorescent fixtures in a collar-tie box that hides the fixtures but casts soft, diffuse light upward.

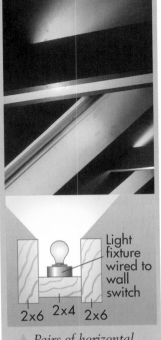

▲ Pairs of horizontal collar ties can conceal lighting fixtures. An open bottom tie casts light up and down (above).With a solid bottom, the light is cast upward (below).

When light is cast upward and reflects off the ceiling, it creates a soft, warm glow. You can install collar-tie lights even if your roof structure does not require collar ties. Build in two closely placed beams that anchor to opposite walls, and install the light fixtures. Attach the beams at regular intervals along the length of the room.

Track lights are a good option for attics because they attach easily to sloped ceilings and can serve as both ambient and task lighting.

Recessed lights placed in sloped ceilings have potential problems. First, they cast light at an awkward angle instead of creating the general downlighting that they are intended to provide. Also, the insulation must be kept 3 inches away from recessed light fixtures. If it's placed directly against a recessed lighting fixture, insulation may overheat and start a fire. Creating holes in the insulation for the lights reduces the energy efficiency of the attic insulation. Only fixtures rated IC (insulated ceiling) can safely come into contact with insulation materials. And, the depth of the roof rafters may make it impossible to install recessed lights. Be sure to include floor, desk, or table lamps in your lighting plan. Movable lamps allow flexibility and are easily rearranged when you move other furnishings. Include plenty of electrical outlets to give you options for adding and moving lamps. Place one outlet on each wall over 2 feet long. And no point along any wall should be more than 6 feet from an electrical outlet.

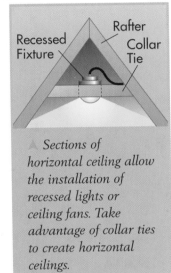

▲ Sections of horizontal ceiling allow the installation of recessed lights or ceiling fans. Take advantage of collar ties to create horizontal ceilings.

Ceiling Fans

You can install a ceiling fan in your attic room as long as you have enough headroom. The minimum requirement for headroom underneath the bottom of a ceiling fan is usually 80 inches. If you are installing a ceiling fan in a peaked ceiling, you'll need to account for the width of the blades. Allow several inches on either side for blade clearance.

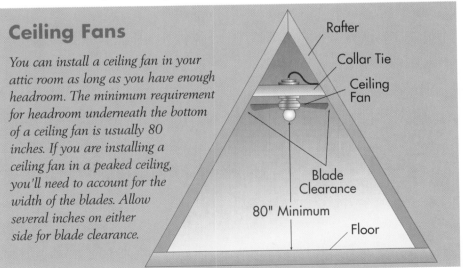

Heating and Cooling
Attic Spaces

Because warm air rises, it is easier to heat attics than it is to cool them. If your home has a central forced-air or a hot-water heating system, you probably can extend it to serve the attic, too. Locate ducts and pipes behind attic knee walls or create a chase—an enclosed area that houses mechanical systems—in an inconspicuous location such as a closet. Even if you can extend your home's system, however, it may no longer work efficiently. Typically, the thermostat used to regulate indoor temperatures is located at a first- or ground-level location—often a considerable vertical distance from attic rooms. This distance could produce a temperature difference of 10 to 15 degrees, meaning that while some portions of the house are comfortable, the attic is not. To correct this problem, you can either add supplemental heating and cooling devices, or you can put the attic on its own thermostat.

Adding Supplemental Heating and Cooling

You'll find a variety of products that work well to provide supplemental heating and cooling to attics. They are relatively small, lightweight appliances that are fairly inconspicuous. Each has a built-in thermostat and temperature-control settings. Electrical heaters can put considerable demands upon your home's electrical system. Consult with a heating and cooling expert or a licensed electrician about whether your supplemental heater or air conditioner needs its own electrical circuit.

■ Baseboard electric heaters come in lengths of 4 or 6 feet and use normal household electrical current. Plug them into a wall outlet or hard-wire them to an electrical circuit. Baseboard heaters are quiet, efficient, and generally easy to conceal.

■ Electric wall heaters have built-in fans to distribute heat and are small enough to fit into most knee walls. Wall heaters use normal household current but must be hard-wired into your home's circuits.

Suggested Total R-Values for Attics

Use the chart below to determine R-value ratings for attic ceilings in your region of the country.

Zone	R-Value
1	19
2	30
3	30
4	30
5	38
6	38
7	38
8	49
9	49
10	55

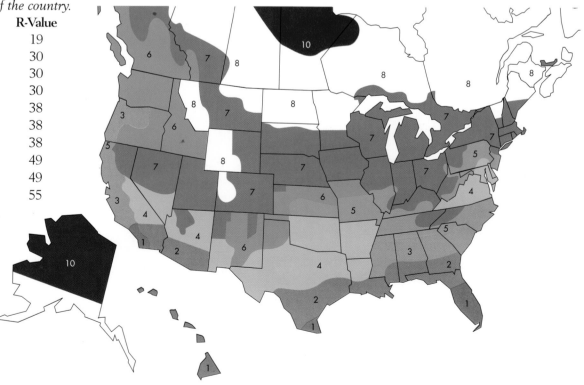

■ Portable air conditioners, sometimes called window air conditioners, are good at providing supplemental cooling. Before purchasing a window unit, measure the square footage of your rooms. Window units generally include ratings that indicate the square footage they can effectively cool. Place these units in a window or in an opening created just for them—so they won't obstruct daylight or views—and install them securely.

■ Ductless heat pumps can function for both heating and cooling. They have two major components—an indoor air handler and an outdoor compressor. They connect to each other with a refrigerant-carrying line that can be up to 160 feet long. Because the refrigerant line requires a hole 3 inches in diameter or less, ductless heat pumps are ideal for those conversion projects that require supplemental heating and cooling. They are also excellent as an independent source of heating and cooling for rooms that are isolated on their own thermostat.

Isolating Attic Rooms on a Separate Thermostat

Isolating attic rooms on a dedicated thermostat allows adjustment of temperature regardless of the temperature of other parts of the home. To create temperature zones within a single structure, the isolated areas must have doors that close them off from other rooms. Isolating works best if each zone is separated from neighboring zones with fiberglass insulation installed in wall, floor, and ceiling cavities. Insulating the independent zones helps increase the energy efficiency of your home by allowing you to regulate temperatures as needed. For example, if a spare attic bedroom is unused during winter, you can turn down its thermostat to conserve energy. When planning separate temperature zones in your home, you should seek the advice of a qualified heating and cooling contractor.

Usually, up to three separate zones can develop using an existing forced-air heating system. The retrofitting consists of extending ducts into new rooms, then adding thermostatically controlled, motorized dampers to the existing ductwork system to control air flow into each zone. Expect to pay between $1,500 and $2,500 to add a zone system to the existing forced-air heating network.

Insulating Attics

For conserving energy, insulating attic rooms is vital. Your goal is to install the optimal R-value for your home, and that depends on the climate in which you live. The United States Department of Energy (DOE) has developed guidelines for R-values for 10 different zones in the United States and Canada (see chart, opposite page). It's possible that local building codes require more insulation than the DOE guidelines. Your contractor should know the recommendations for your area. To find out, ask your local building department or commission.

Encouraging Natural House Ventilation

In good weather, take advantage of attic rooms by opening your house to the natural ventilation that occurs as warm air rises. This process encourages air circulation throughout your home and makes the house feel comfortable even in moderately hot weather. Start by opening attic windows and skylights. Close windows on intermediate levels. Open windows on the lowest level on the shaded side of your home. Cooler air from lower levels replaces warm air that exits attic openings.

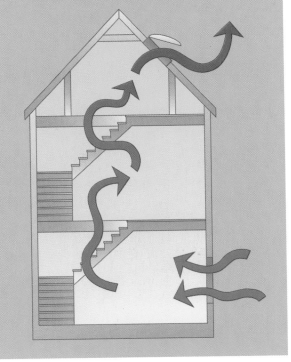

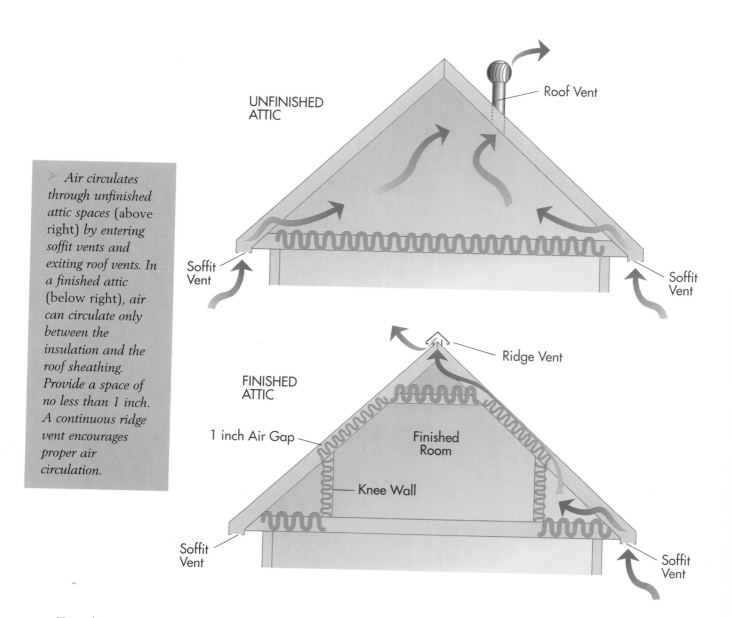

UNFINISHED ATTIC

Roof Vent

Soffit Vent

Soffit Vent

Air circulates through unfinished attic spaces (above right) by entering soffit vents and exiting roof vents. In a finished attic (below right), air can circulate only between the insulation and the roof sheathing. Provide a space of no less than 1 inch. A continuous ridge vent encourages proper air circulation.

Ridge Vent

FINISHED ATTIC

1 inch Air Gap

Finished Room

Knee Wall

Soffit Vent

Soffit Vent

To achieve recommended insulation R-values, you may need to construct knee walls from 2×6 stock rather than from 2×4s. From behind, fully insulate any cabinets, shelves, or drawers built into the knee walls.

When insulating attic spaces, take care to avoid obstructing your attic's passive ventilation system. If the system does not function properly, warm moisture-laden air from your home's interior could migrate to cold attic spaces and form condensation. If severe enough, this condensation could damage roof framing and sheathing.

Your attic's passive ventilation system draws air in through soffit vents that are placed in the eaves of your home, then exhausts the air through metal roof vents or screened openings in the gable ends

of the roof. This naturally occurring ventilation process takes place because warm air is buoyant and flows upward.

Do not allow insulation to block soffit vents, roof vents, or the path between the two. This is especially critical at the sloped portion of your roof. Even though the spaces between roof rafters are filled with insulation, there must be at least a 1-inch air gap between the insulation and the roof sheathing to allow for air flow.

To ensure proper ventilation when converting attics to living spaces for you and your family, you may find that it's necessary to replace roof vent caps with a continuous ridge vent that allows each space between pairs of rafters to "breathe." You also may need to install additional soffit vents.

A ridge vent offers a continuous pathway for air to escape from attics. It lets air out without allowing rain or debris in. Ridge vents require professional installation. (From CertainTeed)

Insulating Against Noise

Noise enters a room in much the same manner as air—through cracks and openings. If you want attic rooms to be quiet, you'll need to provide them with tight-fitting doors that help eliminate noise. If your attic room has a stairwell that opens to rooms below, consider installing a door at the bottom of the stairs. Add a threshold and fit your door with a weatherproof sweep to prevent noise from entering underneath the door. Also, add weather stripping to the door jamb.

To reduce sound that passes through the attic floor from rooms below (and vice-versa), install a carpet and pad. A wall-to-wall carpet can cut sound transmission by almost 40 percent. If you will have access to floor joists, take the opportunity to fill the cavities with fiberglass insulation. Installing 3½-inch fiberglass batts can reduce the transmission of noise by more than 50 percent.

Another effective but more expensive way to reduce sound transmission is to install additional drywall to the ceilings in areas directly below attic rooms. For more effective sound reduction, screw the drywall to resilient metal channels. They help reduce noise transmission by flexing slightly to absorb vibrations. Resilient channels are usually installed at right angles to joists and studs. For additional sound deadening, use ⅝-inch drywall instead of conventional ½-inch.

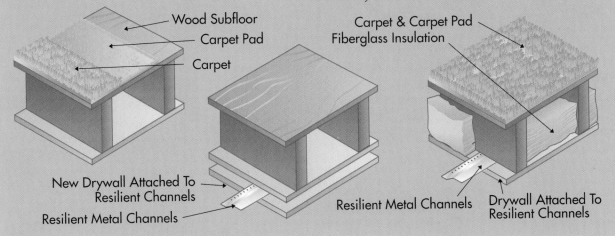

Wood Subfloor
Carpet Pad
Carpet
New Drywall Attached To Resilient Channels
Resilient Metal Channels

Carpet & Carpet Pad
Fiberglass Insulation
Resilient Metal Channels
Drywall Attached To Resilient Channels

Adding an Outdoor Living Area

Creating an outdoor living area for your attic rooms is a great way to enjoy a morning cup of coffee, entertain friends, or just sit and daydream. No matter what you call it—deck, balcony, or porch—an outdoor living area is a cost-effective way to add another dimension to your attic living area. An attic deck can provide a code-compliant safety egress or an outside entrance to attic rooms—an especially convenient feature for in-law apartments or home offices where clients are expected to visit.

Gaining access to your deck is a primary consideration. Decks attached to the gable ends are ideal because a doorway usually is relatively easy to construct at a gable location. If your attic has no easy access to the area where you'd like to put your deck, you'll need to create one. Typically, you will need a dormer large enough to accommodate a doorway. While the construction of a dormer is straightforward, it will add a considerable expense to your costs.

The construction of an attic deck is similar to most decks, except that it has longer support posts. When designing an attic deck, you need to be aware if the deck will affect rooms below by obstructing daylight, or by putting support posts in an awkward location, such as in front of a

▶ *A big deck cozies up to attic rooms and provides plenty of getaway space. The deck is supported by a portion of the house with a flat roof and can drain directly to the roofing material below.*

This master suite was built over a garage, and it includes a private deck that is actually the second of two levels—there's another deck directly underneath. The arrangement allows one foundation for both decks and prevents posts supporting the upper deck from looking too long and spindly.

window or doorway. Because an attic deck will become a prominent architectural feature of your home, it should look as if it was designed to fit with the style of your home—not just tacked on as an afterthought. This is especially true if your deck will include an outside stairway. Exterior stairways leading to upper-level rooms can be long and ungainly. Try to design a stairway that is graceful and unobtrusive.

Most outdoor decks have typical deck flooring—wood planks with gaps between them for drainage. If you prefer a solid floor such as quarry tile, you'll need a waterproof subfloor as a base. These kinds of subfloors usually include layers of relatively expensive materials, such as marine-grade plywood that are covered with a waterproof coating. Also, solid exterior floors must slope away from the house at the rate of at least ¼-inch per foot to prevent rain and melted snow from entering the structure. Solid roofs should drain properly and include a system of gutters and downspouts.

Outdoor decks must conform to all zoning laws and building codes. To ensure your project goes smoothly, you'll need to submit your plans to your local building department or commission to obtain a building permit. During construction, your project will be examined by a representative from your building department to ensure the deck is built according to approved plans. When planning your deck, keep these code and safety points in mind:

■ Attic decks must conform to setback requirements—the distance from neighboring property lines where new construction is forbidden. A typical setback requirement is 15 feet along the sides of a property and 45 feet front and back. Your local zoning laws may vary and should be determined before you begin planning.

■ Build your upper-level deck strong—with safety as a primary goal. Typically, railings must be at least 36 inches high and balusters spaced no more than 4 inches apart, measured on-centers. Check building codes for the requirements in your neighborhood.

■ Most deck posts are supported on foundation piers—poured-concrete posts that typically extend more than 3 feet underground. Before digging begins, you'll need to check with your local utility and cable television companies to make sure your piers stay clear of buried cables, pipes, and wires.

▶ *Snuggled up to the trees, this attic balcony brings upper-level rooms in direct contact with nature. The tile floor is set in a concrete subfloor pitched to drain away from the structure. The iron railings were custom-made for this project.*

Bathrooms

A new bathroom is always a welcome addition to a house and a good investment. If you should sell your home, you are likely to recover about 90 percent of the costs of a bathroom addition. Usually, an attic bathroom is an essential element of an apartment, master suite, or guest bedroom. Even a small bathroom is a wonderful convenience that saves having to trudge up and down stairs.

An attic bathroom doesn't have to be large. A space 30 inches wide and 75 inches long—just 16 square feet—is adequate for a toilet and a sink. If you wish to include a shower or bathtub, you'll need a space about 5 feet wide and 7 feet long—only about 35 square feet. Building codes allow ceiling heights of 84 inches for bathrooms—6 inches lower than for other living areas. This can be an important factor in attics where ceiling height may be restricted by sloped ceilings.

The size of an attic bathroom can vary, but bathrooms that include heavy items such as cast-iron tubs and tile floors need to have especially strong floor framing. Have your floor framing inspected by an architect, structural engineer, or other qualified

▶ This top-of-the-house master suite features a bedroom at one end of the attic and this stylish bathroom at the other. Patterned wallpaper and built-in cabinetry give an elegant appearance. The tub has been snuggled in beneath the sloped ceiling to conserve space.

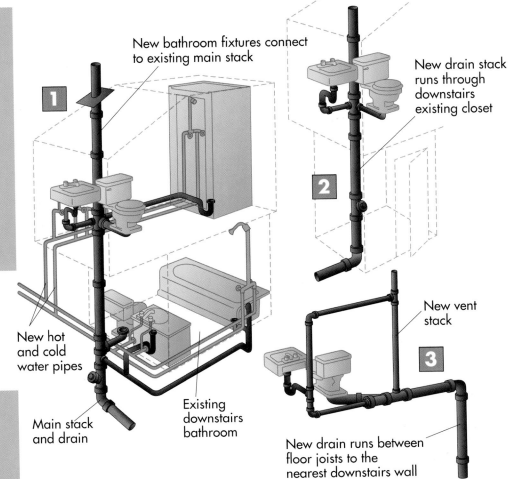

New bathroom fixtures connect to existing main stack

New drain stack runs through downstairs existing closet

1

2

New vent stack

3

New hot and cold water pipes

Main stack and drain

Existing downstairs bathroom

New drain runs between floor joists to the nearest downstairs wall

professional to see if joists need to be strengthened to accommodate your plans. Don't forget that those cast-iron tubs that look so inviting on the showroom floor are extremely heavy, and are difficult to carry up stairs. If your plans include a cast-iron tub, make sure your stairway has plenty of room to maneuver such a cumbersome item.

Extending hot and cold water supply pipes to a new bathroom is usually a simple matter of splicing into existing lines. The most critical factor in locating an attic bathroom is tying into existing drains and vent stacks. All bathroom fixtures must drain into the main drain—usually a 3- or 4-inch diameter pipe that exits the house through the basement floor. Access to the main drain is gained by tying into some point along the existing drain system. For this reason, it is usually easiest to position a new bathroom directly over an existing bathroom or kitchen. That way, all drain and supply pipes are readily accessible, and you can make connections to other rooms of your house with a minimum of cost and disruption. Plumbing lines should never be made to run in unheated portions of the house, such as the space behind a knee wall.

Fixtures such as tubs or showers that drain into floor drains present another problem—their drain lines require a certain amount of slope or "fall" to function properly. This slope limits the horizontal distance you can position a tub or shower away from an existing drain line. Also, drain lines should run parallel to floor joists so that cutting the joists is unnecessary. One solution is to place tubs or showers on a raised platform. The platform helps conceal horizontal runs of drain pipe and allows greater flexibility in positioning tubs or showers. Although codes allow lower headroom clearances for bath-

rooms than for other rooms, you'll still need to check to make sure headroom is adequate. Another solution is to install the new drain lines so that they run through an inconspicuous location in one of the rooms below the attic. A closet is a good choice.

If you are considering adding a new bathroom to your attic, it's wise to consult an architect, builder, or licensed plumber. Be sure to obtain a full estimate for the work before proceeding.

> This old Victorian farmhouse offered lots of space, and a generous attic was readily converted into a master suite. The tub was left open to the large dressing room that includes several cherished antiques, including a grand walnut sideboard and a cane-backed chair.

An attic bedroom gained a whimsical bathroom with the addition of a raised platform that conceals new plumbing lines and avoided the need for opening up walls.

This 4x6-foot half bath doesn't take up much room yet features a toilet, vanity sink, storage, and plenty of great style. The wood floor is painted to match the overall color scheme. The skylight offer generous amounts of daylight yet preserves privacy.

Attic Storage That Works

Storage is an important element in any room design. Fortunately, the unusual shape of attic spaces is well-suited to creating unique and clever storage solutions.

The basic building block of attic storage is the knee wall. Typically, knee walls are no less than 3 or 4 feet high. This still leaves a considerable amount of empty space behind them, which is then available for built-in storage and closets. Locate shelves, cabinets, and drawers in knee walls to create storage that does not use up any living space. Use casters on items such as bins or beds which you then can tuck away in knee-wall cubbyholes when not in use. For energy efficiency and comfort, enclose and insulate knee wall compartments.

Because they are low, knee walls also make ideal locations for a variety of furnishings such as desks, tables, bookshelves, and chests of drawers. Placed against knee walls, these items do not intrude into

Cleverly designed to fit the slope of the roof, this shelf unit fits neatly alongside a slanted ceiling and takes advantage of every inch of space.

Adequate storage was one of the goals of this attic conversion. A narrow dormer window was fitted with a window seat that features built-in shelves, and cavities behind knee walls were made accessible with large doors.

◀ *Stairwells create opportunities for storage. Instead of an open railing, this stairway is guarded by deep bookshelves. In addition, the partition wall at the head of the stairs features more shelves for displaying books and knicknacks.*

traffic areas. When considering furnishings for your attic rooms, keep in mind the height of any knee walls and how you can position furniture.

Interior partition walls for attic rooms are often odd-shaped because of sloped ceilings. While partition walls may not make good locations for pieces of tall furniture, you can custom-design them to include built-in shelves that make ideal storage for books and accessories. If your stairway includes a railing that surrounds the access opening, consider a solid railing that features built-in bookshelves facing the attic space.

> *Tall side walls are all that's needed to create full-sized attic closets. This generous closet features standard bi-fold doors that don't intrude upon the available space.*

Opening Up Attics With Dormer Windows

Adding a dormer window is a great way to improve the architectural interest of ordinary exteriors and to open up attic rooms to light and ventilation. Best of all, you can increase the amount of headroom in your attic and add valuable living space. If your attic does not meet the code requirement for minimum amount of headroom—more than 50 percent of the living area must have at least 90 inches from the finished floor to the ceiling—adding dormers may help you gain the space you need. Even small dormers expand attics visually and provide useful spaces that you can fit with window seats, small desks—or leave

them open as getaway nooks—a feature children find especially delightful.

Dormers resemble small houses, complete with walls, siding, windows, trim, and roofs. Generally, they mimic the existing style of the house, and are likely to feature similar window shapes, roof pitch, and architectural details. Dormers typically intersect the roof below the highest point of the structure—the main ridge.

Because dormers can alter exterior appearance dramatically, they should be well-proportioned. A well-designed dormer is big enough to be worth the expense of construction, yet not so large as to overwhelm the architectural integrity of your home. Two or three smaller dormers, carefully spaced across a roof, are generally more appealing than one enormous dormer. Dormers appear in almost as many shapes and configurations as there are architectural styles, but there are two basic types—shed and gable.

▼ *Dormer windows may have only two basic configurations, but they feature variations that will match a variety of architectural styles. In eyebrow dormers the windows admit light but do not open.*

DORMERS

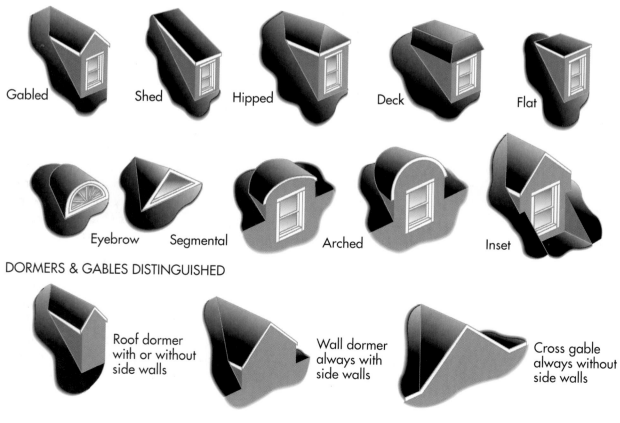

Gabled · Shed · Hipped · Deck · Flat

Eyebrow · Segmental · Arched · Inset

DORMERS & GABLES DISTINGUISHED

Roof dormer with or without side walls

Wall dormer always with side walls

Cross gable always without side walls

▲ *A wide shed dormer fits the style of this shingled cottage. The dormer is part of a remodeling that includes a bay window on the first floor. As an architectural flourish, the bottom of the dormer extends below the eaves.*

Shed Dormers

A shed dormer is the simplest form of dormer window. It features a flat roof whose pitch is slightly less than the main roof. Its uncomplicated shape means that you can construct it more easily than other dormers, and building a shed dormer is more cost-efficient. It usually offers more total headroom than a gable dormer of equal width. Take care with its design, however—large shed dormers tend to look ungainly.

The pitch of a shed dormer roof is independent of the pitch of the main roof of the house, and you will find many angles can be used for a pleasing effect. However, the angle of the roof will affect the amount of headroom available on the inside of the structure—flatter roofs open up more space. When designing, keep in mind that a shed dormer's flat roof requires sufficient pitch to drain properly. Reducing pitch limits the kinds of roofing materials that you can use to cover the structure. Typical asphalt or fiberglass shingles require a minimum pitch of 3 in 12, or 3 inches of vertical fall for every 12 inches of horizontal run. Wood shingles are not recommended on pitches less than 4 in 12. Roof pitches less than 3 in 12 usually require special roofing materials, such as rolled asphalt covered with hot tar or seamless rubber membranes.

Gable Dormers

A gable dormer has a peaked or rounded roof and drains precipitation to either side of a central ridge. The roof structure of a gable dormer is complex and usually more expensive to build than a shed dormer of equal size. Because the roof slants to each side, not all the space under a gable dormer may be high enough to qualify as usable living space according to building codes. Make careful calculations to determine usable living space.

Building Dormers

Dormer construction requires cutting away part of the exterior roof surface, then cutting a number of rafters to create a hole. You must support these rafters must with temporary bracing before you cut them. This is a job that requires opening the roof to the elements, so you're better off to plan the work for warm weather. Your builder should cover the roof openings when work is not in progress— typically with sheets of plastic temporarily secrued in place with thin strips of wood called battens. Before work begins, it's a good idea to find out from your contractor the person you should call if severe weather damages the temporary covering. Prepare yourself by having at least two emergency numbers available. Make sure the contractor has the proper insurance to cover any damage that may occur due to leakage of the covering, and inspect your contract for clauses that state the contractor is responsible for making any repairs that become necessary.

▶ *Arched dormers, sometimes called barrel-vaulted dormers, create interesting interior ceilings. This dormer ceiling is finished with thin wood strips that accentuate its graceful curves. A round-top window matches the shape of the vault.*

The soaring window of this attic bedroom was accommodated by allowing the top of the dormer to extend past the ceiling. The result creates interesting line contrasts inside the room but still manages to keep most of the ceiling low enough to make the room feel cozy.

Even small dormers offer opportunities for decorative finery. The inside walls of this one feature hand-painted murals. A fabric shade tied up with a big bow and a bouquet of flowers on the inset shelf finish it off with a quiet elegance.

Planning Your
New Space

Good planning helps projects proceed smoothly and keeps costs under control.

A good plan has two basic components—drawings and a budget. First, outline your goals. Imagine how you will use the space, and how elaborate you want the finished space to be. The more detailed your goals, the more likely that you'll be satisfied when the project is complete. For example, your basic goal may be "to add more living space to the house." But be specific. If you plan for comfortable seating for watching television and reading books, if you decide ahead of time for storage for camping gear, or for a quiet place to write cards and letters, then you'll have a much better idea of how to configure the available space. You will know in advance how big storage cabinets should be, what size and kind of furniture to include, and what kinds of lighting you'll need.

➤ Although simple, this attic space shows off many elements of thoughtful planning: roof windows for lighting, a flat section of ceiling for a fan, generous closets, a nook with built-in headboard designed to fit a queen-size bed, and the exposed surface of an existing chimney which becomes a decorative part of the interior.

Next, take accurate measurements of your attic and use grid paper to create a map of the space. Grid paper is provided on pages 94–95 of this book. Drawn as seen from above, this map is called a plan view, and on it you should indicate any existing stairways, windows, dormers, and obstructions, such as vent stacks and chimneys. Remember that many homes were built from blueprints that may still exist. If the builder of your home is in your area and can be contacted, you may be able to obtain a set of blueprints that you can use for planning purposes.

Include a side view of the space, called a section view. Your section view should indicate the slope of the roof, the locations of windows and dormers, and the amount of available headroom. Planning attic rooms assumes you have enough headroom to convert the space to living area. To make sure your attic meets this primary requirement, see "How Do I Know if I Have Enough Headroom?" on page 7.

Managing space with careful planning is essential for small attic rooms. Here, a chair and side table are tucked away under the sloped ceiling. A small shelf built into the gable-end wall provides a place to display decorative items. The window alcove features a built-in storage cabinet for extra pillows and blankets.

It's important to plan for the future locations of stairways. Some older homes and one-and-a-half story houses often have stairways that lead to attic spaces. If so, you'll need to determine if the existing stairs meet code requirements for safety or if they can be readily converted for compliance and adequacy. See "Finding Room for Stairs," on pages 54–57. If no stairs exist, creating them will be a major focus of your project. You'll need a floor plan of the level directly below your attic so you can locate a place for the stairway to begin. This may be the most difficult part of planning your project, and it's a good idea to consult with an architect or other design professional to discuss possible solutions and costs (see "Working With a Design Professional," opposite page). On your plan view, you'll need to sketch in your attic living area—that will be the portion that has enough headroom.

Typically, the living area is separated from non-living areas by knee walls. Remember that spaces behind knee walls are usable for storage. Draw in any partition walls, new dormers, and other changes to the livable area. Include the locations of doors and windows, and indicate where new electrical outlets, light switches, and light fixtures will go. To give yourself an idea of how this process can work, see "Mapping the Changes," page 82.

Once you have your plans on paper, visualize the materials and furniture you'll add to complete your conversion. Cutouts of popular furnishings, appliances, and fixtures are available on pages 91–93 and are made to fit the scale of the grid paper. Once you've specified your finish materials, you are ready to estimate costs for items and to begin establishing a budget (see "What Will it Cost?" pages 96–109).

Working with a Design Professional

The job of a professional designer is to create a space that meets your needs. A professional's expertise and experience allows him or her to offer fresh ideas, anticipate code restrictions, and deal with unusual problems. If the cost of hiring a pro seems prohibitive, consider that professionals can help save on overall costs by contributing to the efficiency of the project, organizing and managing work flow, and helping to avoid expensive mistakes. Many pros are willing to work as consultants for an hourly fee.

When working with a professional, good communication is key to achieving your goals. To help express your ideas, start a clipping folder. Use it to keep articles and photographs cut from magazines that show ideas and design details that appeal to you. Add product brochures or advertisements that you can share with your designer. A good designer is interested in your lifestyle and should ask questions about how you live, your daily routine, and your project goals.

Three types of design professionals are available for helping work on an attic project. Although they have specialized areas of expertise, most professionals are well-versed in all phases of design and can help create a comprehensive plan.

■ Architects work primarily with structure and reorganization of space. They are familiar with many types of building materials, finishes, and appliances, and have thorough knowledge of structural, electrical, plumbing, heating, ventilation, and air conditioning systems. Plans that include structural changes to your house and that need to be reviewed by your local building and planning commission should bear the stamp of a professional architect or structural engineer. Architects charge a percentage of the total cost of the project, usually 10 to 15 percent. If you hire them on an hourly basis, they charge $50 to $125 per hour. For a listing of architects in your area, look in the Yellow Pages of your phone directory, or try the internet search engine offered by the American Institute of Architects at http://www.e-architect.com/reference/home.asp.

■ Interior designers work with colors, wall finishes, fabrics, floor coverings, furnishings, lighting, and accessories to personalize a space and create a look that appeals to their clients. Increasingly, interior designers are familiar with building codes and structural requirements and can make recommendations for placement of partition walls, plumbing hookups, electrical outlets, and architectural details, such as built-in storage units, moldings, door styles and sizes, and windows. If necessary, however, project plans must be approved by the local building and planning commission. Structural changes require the stamp of a structural engineer or registered architect. Extensive remodeling projects may be subject to periodic inspection by the local building inspector. Interior designers certified by the American Society of Interior Designers (ASID) must demonstrate an ongoing knowledge of materials, building codes, government regulations, safety standards, and the latest products. For more information, visit the ASID web site at http://www.asid.org.

■ Design/build teams offer complete project management from initial design to completion of construction. Their involvement ensures that they are thoroughly familiar with the building methods and techniques specified by the project plan. Design/build teams may not offer the services of a registered architect. Therefore, structural modifications will require the approval of an architect or structural engineer. Design/build teams rarely offer interior design services.

Mapping The Changes

Perfect the design for your new attic rooms using a three-stage process: First, draw up a plan of the existing space, then sketch in all the anticipated modifications. and finally, add furnishings. Even if you're planning to hire an architect or interior designer, sketch your preliminary ideas. Your sketches will serve as the basis for additional planning and will help you express your ideas to your designer.

The map of your existing attic should be drawn to scale with all details noted (see page 78 for tips on doing a plan view). Make several photocopies so you can test a variety of design options and solutions on paper.

Once you decide on a general layout for the space, use the "Room-Arranging Kit" (see pages 90-95) to plan for room furnishings. If you can't get the pieces to fit, go back to step two and make modifications to room sizes and configurations.

To give you an idea of how the process works, study this section to see how plans evolve.

Adding a Study

The floor plan and style of this house is typical of many homes built during the last 20 years. Although there are no stairs leading to the attic, the roof features a steep 12-in-12 pitch and offers plenty of headroom for the conversion plan. The main problem—finding room for stairs—is solved by devoting a portion of the large, second-floor master bedroom to the construction of a new stairway. The new, 3-foot-wide stairway is placed near the existing hallway so that it is readily accessible by all members of the household. The master bedroom retains generous 16x14 proportions and receives a new passage door.

In the attic, usable space is increased by the addition of an 11-foot-wide gable-end dormer window. Because of the roof configuration there were no windows within the existing attic space. The dormer

solves the problem by bringing daylight to the new attic room through a pair of double-hung windows. Furnished with comfortable chairs, bookshelves, and lamps, the dormer becomes a cozy reading nook. In the remaining space, available daylight is augmented by the addition of a 2x4-foot skylight that opens to create cross ventilation within the room. A small closet located at the head of the stairs provides addition general storage for the household.

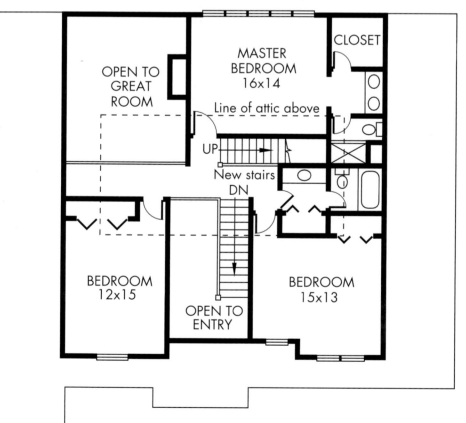

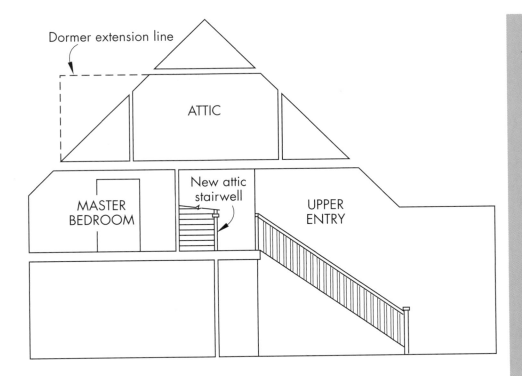

Dormer extension line

ATTIC

MASTER BEDROOM

New attic stairwell

UPPER ENTRY

A revised floor plan for the upper level (opposite) shows where a new stairway is fitted inside an existing master bedroom. The outline indicates the usable attic space directly above. A section view (left) shows the placement of knee walls, a new ceiling, and a dormer window. A final plan for the space (below) indicates possible furniture placement for the finished attic room.

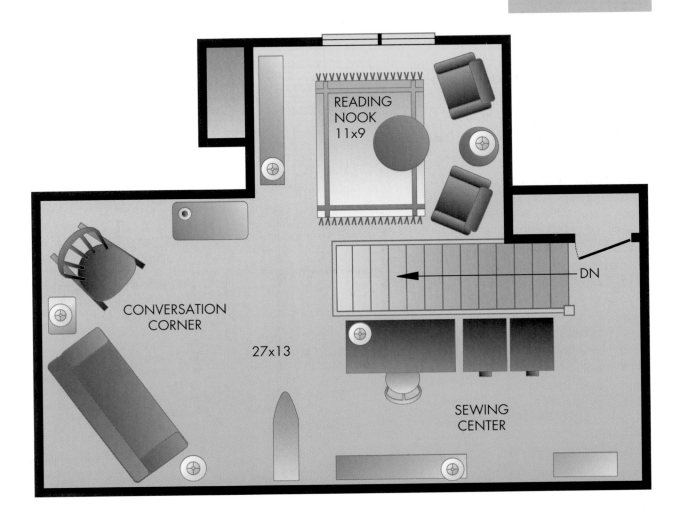

READING NOOK 11x9

CONVERSATION CORNER

27x13

DN

SEWING CENTER

An Office Over the Garage

A two-car garage offers a generous amount of unused attic space. It is a good location for a private office apart from everyday household activities. The garage in this example is even more tempting because it does not share a common wall with the main house—it is separated by a single-story enclosed breezeway used as a mudroom and laundry. To access the garage attic, the breezeway was reconfigured, shrinking the mudroom and laundry areas to gain enough space for a 3-foot-wide stair-

way. Notice that the stairway is positioned so that it doesn't interfere with the existing entry door in the front of the breezeway.

In the attic, the drop-down stairway is removed and the joists strengthened to carry the weight of heavy bookshelves, filing cabinets, and everyday use. The spaces between the joists are filled with insulation so the area can be heated and cooled independently of the garage below. The roofline over the single-story breezeway is reconfigured to align with the existing roofline of the garage, allowing enough headroom that a small but convenient bathroom can adjoin the office. The bathroom, positioned above mudroom and laundry facilities, has access to water lines, drain pipes, and vent stacks.

To provide daylight and ventilation, two small gable-end dormer windows are added to the attic space. An existing window located in the gable end of the garage is enlarged to ensure a safety egress.

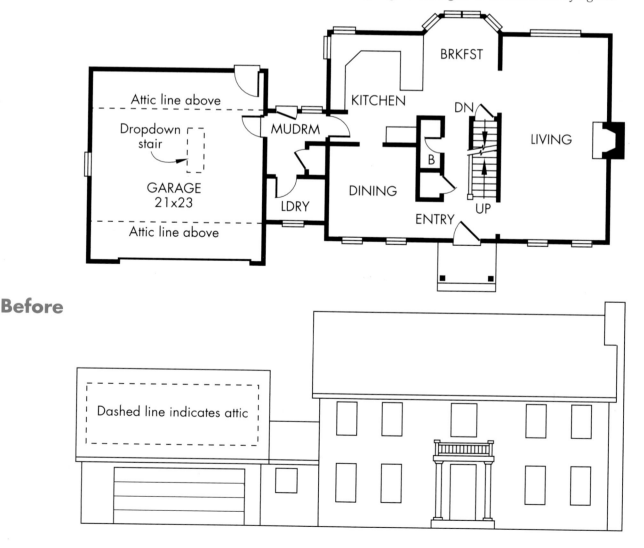

Before

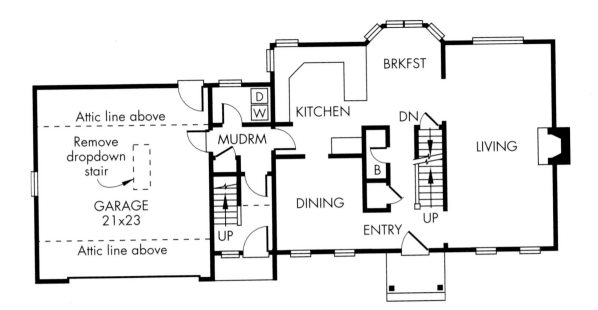

Attic line above

Remove dropdown stair

GARAGE 21x23

Attic line above

UP

MUDRM

DW

KITCHEN

BRKFST

DN

UP

B

LIVING

DINING

ENTRY

After

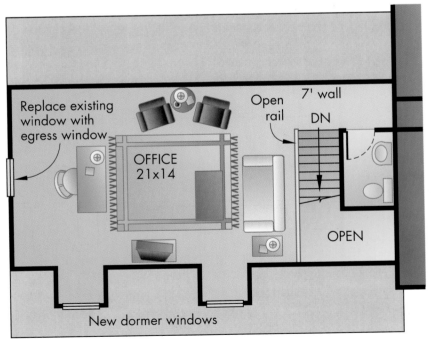

Replace existing window with egress window

OFFICE 21x14

Open rail

7' wall

DN

OPEN

New dormer windows

To access the available space over the garage, this design took the existing breezeway and used it as access for a stairway. Raising the roof over the breezeway accommodates a small bathroom. The changes are readily apparent by viewing the exterior elevations of the house before (opposite) and after (above) the alterations.

A Master Suite in an Unused Attic

Like many story-and-a-half homes, this house featured an attic space that was accessible by an existing stairway but was never configured for modern living. Rather than move, the owners decided to capitalize on this space by creating an attic suite, thereby freeing up a downstairs bedroom for their growing family.

The renovation features improvements to a number of existing features. The stairway is widened for safety and better accessibility. At the top of the stairs, an existing furnace flue is moved slightly and hidden within a wall that is built alongside the new stairway. The roofline of an existing dormer window is raised, and its interior walls lengthened to gain the space necessary for a centrally located bathroom. Notice that the bathroom has two doorways—one doorway provides access to the main portion of the master suite, and the other doorway leads to a generous closet/storage area. The closet is formed by reconfiguring existing knee walls near the top of the stairs and using the walls of the central bathroom core to help enclose the space. This closet/storage area has a second access door located at the stair landing.

To give the main room of the suite some style, an existing window facing the front of the house was enlarged as a bumpout dormer. The new dormer gives the room an architecturally interesting feature and also provides code-compliant safety egress required for attic sleeping areas. As an added treat, a zero-clearance gas fireplace was added next to the bathroom wall. The fireplace is lightweight and requires no structural modifications to the floor. A small-diameter vent pipe runs up through the roof and exhausts the fireplace to the outside.

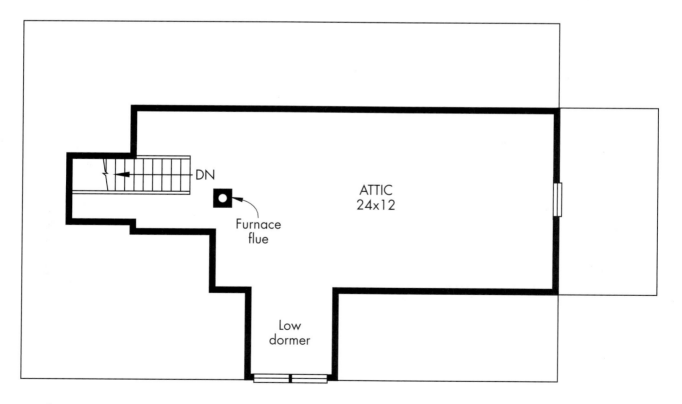

DN

Furnace flue

ATTIC
24x12

Low dormer

Before

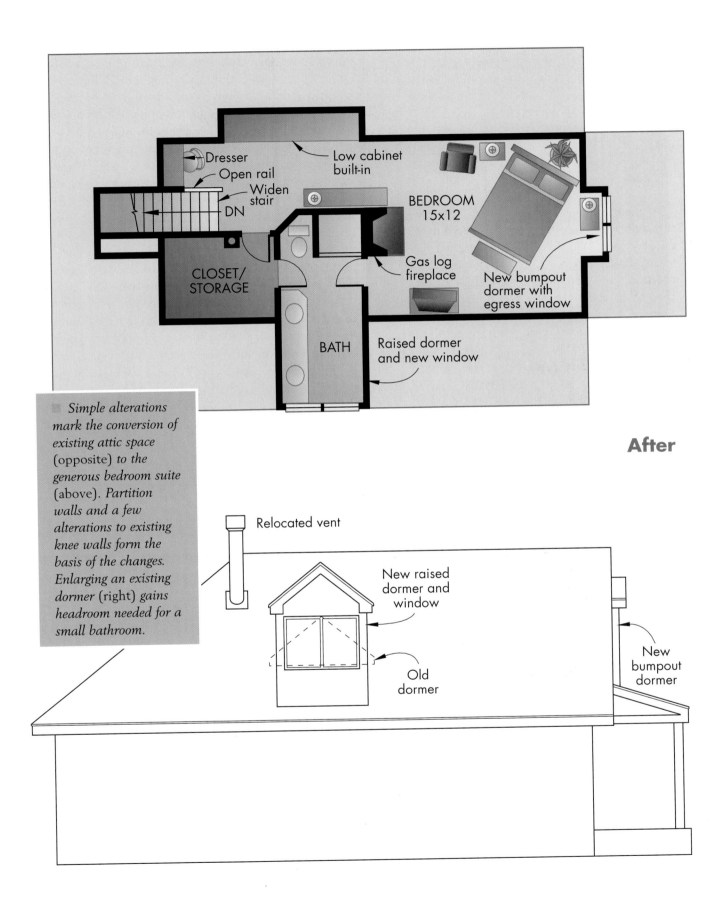

Dresser

Open rail

Widen stair

DN

Low cabinet built-in

BEDROOM 15x12

Gas log fireplace

New bumpout dormer with egress window

CLOSET/ STORAGE

BATH

Raised dormer and new window

After

Simple alterations mark the conversion of existing attic space (opposite) to the generous bedroom suite (above). Partition walls and a few alterations to existing knee walls form the basis of the changes. Enlarging an existing dormer (right) gains headroom needed for a small bathroom.

Relocated vent

New raised dormer and window

Old dormer

New bumpout dormer

An Apartment With a Private Entrance

This house had generous proportions and a usable attic with an existing stairway. But when the homeowners decided to convert the attic to an apartment for their active mother, they wanted to create a separate, private entrance. The solution required modifications to the floor plan of the main level to accommodate an additional stairway. The additional space was gained by reconfiguring a mudroom and bedroom closet into smaller areas. The new stairway also includes a door to the garage. The existing stairway remains intact to provide inside access to the main portion of the house.

In the apartment, the three-quarter bathroom is located directly above the kitchen to provide access to water supply lines, drain pipes, and vent stacks. The 2-inch drain line for the kitchenette had to be run through an existing wall to tie into the drain lines available in the downstairs laundry.

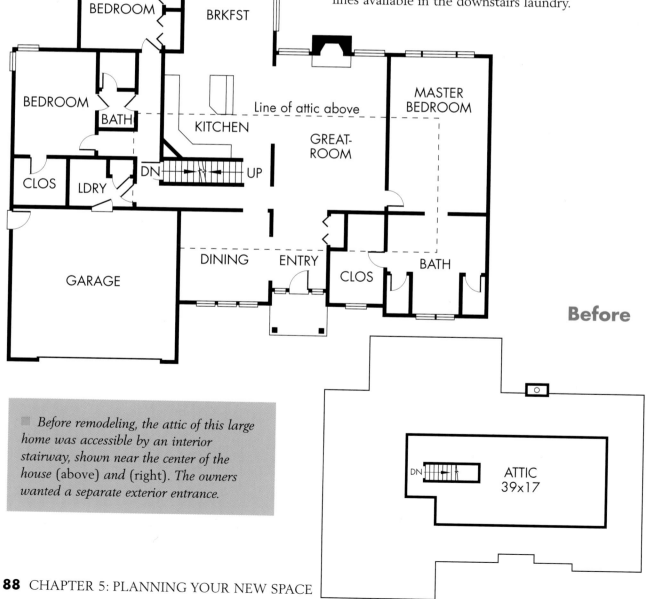

Before remodeling, the attic of this large home was accessible by an interior stairway, shown near the center of the house (above) and (right). The owners wanted a separate exterior entrance.

Before

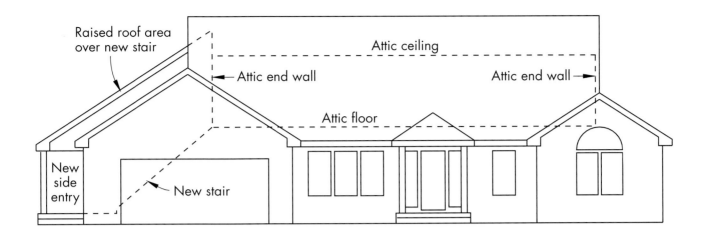

Raised roof area over new stair

Attic ceiling

Attic end wall

Attic end wall

Attic floor

New side entry

New stair

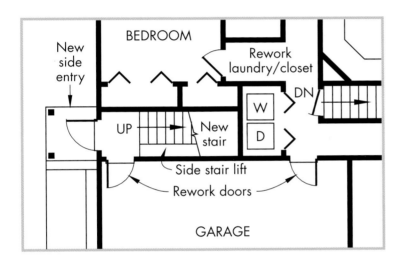

BEDROOM

New side entry

Rework laundry/closet

DN

W

D

UP

New stair

Side stair lift

Rework doors

GARAGE

The solution, shown in the detail (left), uses a portion of an existing closet to bring the new stairway down alongside an interior garage wall. Because of set-back restrictions, however, the new entrance could not project too much from the side of the house. Therefore, a portion of the roof over the stairway (shown above) had to be raised to gain the required headroom.

After

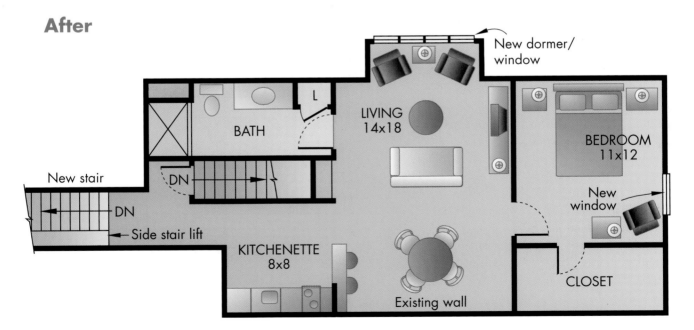

New dormer/ window

L

BATH

LIVING
14x18

BEDROOM
11x12

New stair

DN

DN

Side stair lift

New window

KITCHENETTE
8x8

CLOSET

Existing wall

Room Arranging Kit

The key to creating an inviting, usable space is good placement of furnishings. Think about how you plan to use the space and choose the pieces—both furniture you have and items you'll add—needed to make the space work. Using the Room-Arranging Kit on the following pages, work through these steps:

■ *Measure the room.* Plot it on the grid (pages 94-95) or on same-size grid paper. One square equals one foot of floor space. Use the architectural symbols *(right)* to mark doorways, stairs, and the like. Be sure to include all the structural features of the existing space. Using dotted lines, mark key obstructions—such as low ductwork or lights.

■ *Use the furniture templates.* Trace or photocopy the appropriate items from the templates on the following pages, and cut them out with a crafts knife. If you have furniture or special items that need templates, measure them and draw them to the same scale—one square equals one foot—on grid paper.

■ *Find a focal point.* This is the physical cornerstone around which you build a furniture grouping; visually, it's the dramatic element that draw you into a room. If your room doesn't have a natural focus—such as a fireplace or built-in bookcases—substitute a large-scaled or boldly colored accessory or freestanding wall units.

Here are a few tips to help you place furnishings in your new space:

■ *Direct traffic.* If traffic passes through a room, it doesn't have to run through the center. Think of your furnishings as walls or guideposts that can funnel traffic.

■ *Float furnishings.* Pull pieces away from walls into close-knit groupings with major seating no more than 8 feet apart.

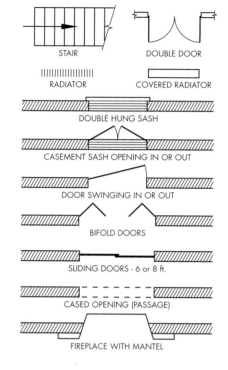

Architectural Symbols

STAIR

DOUBLE DOOR

RADIATOR

COVERED RADIATOR

DOUBLE HUNG SASH

CASEMENT SASH OPENING IN OR OUT

DOOR SWINGING IN OR OUT

BIFOLD DOORS

SLIDING DOORS - 6 or 8 ft.

CASED OPENING (PASSAGE)

FIREPLACE WITH MANTEL

■ *Reshape Space.* Break a long, narrow room into two groupings. If space allows, place a sofa or love seat perpendicular to a long wall to visually widen the space. A diagonal is the longest line through any room, so "widen" a tunnel shape or break up a boxy one by arranging seating pieces on the diagonal.

■ *Keep convenience within reach.* Set a handy resting place—an end table, stack of books, or short cabinet—for drinks or books close to every seat.

■ *Maximize a small room.* Include a large-scale piece, such as an armoire or hefty love seat, for a feeling of grandeur. Use vertical storage in tight spaces.

■ *Fix low ceilings.* "Raise" a low ceiling with floor-to-ceiling window treatments and tall furniture. And allow for ceiling obstructions. Direct traffic away from or around these low-hanging items. (See illustration, *(left)*, for the minimum height requirements.)

Minimum height allowed from finished floor to finished ceiling 7'6"

Indicated the amount of width considered by codes to be liveable area

20'

Upholstered Furniture and Bedding

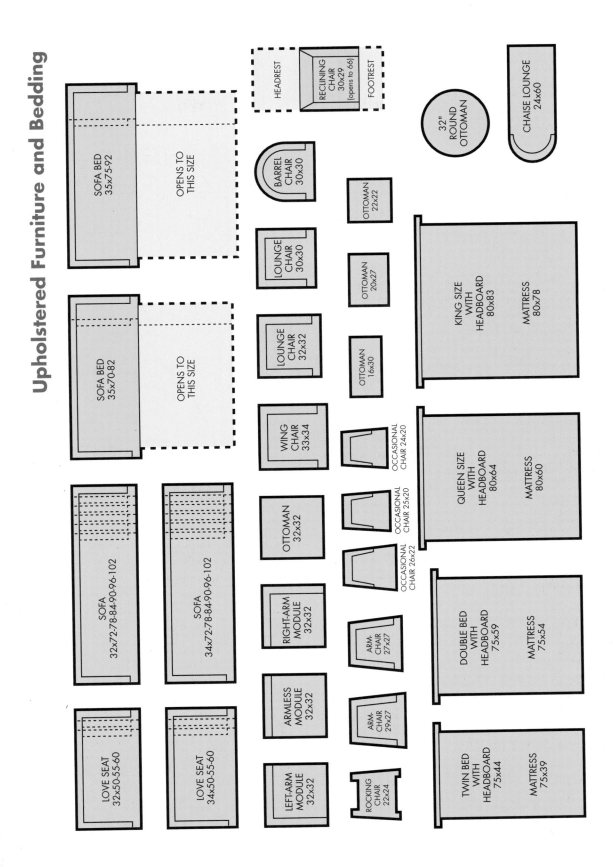

SOFA BED
35x75-92

OPENS TO
THIS SIZE

SOFA BED
35x70-82

OPENS TO
THIS SIZE

SOFA
32x72-78-84-90-96-102

SOFA
34x72-78-84-90-96-102

LOVE SEAT
32x50-55-60

LOVE SEAT
34x50-55-60

HEADREST

RECLINING
CHAIR
30x29
(opens to 66)

FOOTREST

BARREL
CHAIR
30x30

LOUNGE
CHAIR
30x30

LOUNGE
CHAIR
32x32

WING
CHAIR
33x34

OTTOMAN
32x32

RIGHT-ARM
MODULE
32x32

ARMLESS
MODULE
32x32

LEFT-ARM
MODULE
32x32

OTTOMAN
22x22

OTTOMAN
20x27

OTTOMAN
16x30

OCCASIONAL
CHAIR 24x20

OCCASIONAL
CHAIR 25x20

OCCASIONAL
CHAIR 26x22

ARM-
CHAIR
27x27

ARM-
CHAIR
29x27

ROCKING
CHAIR
22x24

32"
ROUND
OTTOMAN

CHAISE LOUNGE
24x60

KING SIZE
WITH
HEADBOARD
80x83

MATTRESS
80x78

QUEEN SIZE
WITH
HEADBOARD
80x64

MATTRESS
80x60

DOUBLE BED
WITH
HEADBOARD
75x59

MATTRESS
75x54

TWIN BED
WITH
HEADBOARD
75x44

MATTRESS
75x39

Room Arranging Kit

Use a photocopier to reproduce these cutout images at 100 percent of their original size. Work with the grid on pages 94-95.

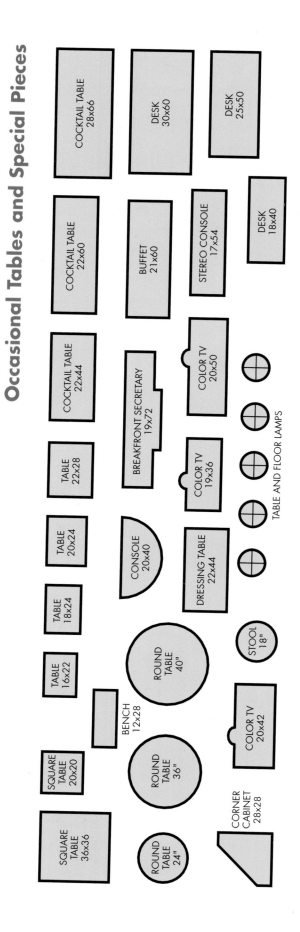

Occasional Tables and Special Pieces

COCKTAIL TABLE 28x66

DESK 30x60

DESK 25x50

COCKTAIL TABLE 22x60

BUFFET 21x60

STEREO CONSOLE 17x54

DESK 18x40

COCKTAIL TABLE 22x44

BREAKFRONT SECRETARY 19x72

COLOR TV 20x50

TABLE 22x28

COLOR TV 19x36

TABLE 20x24

CONSOLE 20x40

DRESSING TABLE 22x44

TABLE AND FLOOR LAMPS

TABLE 18x24

TABLE 16x22

ROUND TABLE 40"

STOOL 18"

BENCH 12x28

SQUARE TABLE 20x20

ROUND TABLE 36"

COLOR TV 20x42

SQUARE TABLE 36x36

ROUND TABLE 24"

CORNER CABINET 28x28

Bathroom Fixtures and Exercise Equipment

48-INCH VANITY

60-INCH VANITY DOUBLE SINK

STANDARD TOILET

ELONGATED TOILET

32-INCH VANITY

3x3 SHOWER ENCLOSURE

BATHTUB

TREADMILL

WEIGHT-LIFTING STATION

STATIONARY BIKE

STAIR-STEPPER

Stairs and Stair Openings

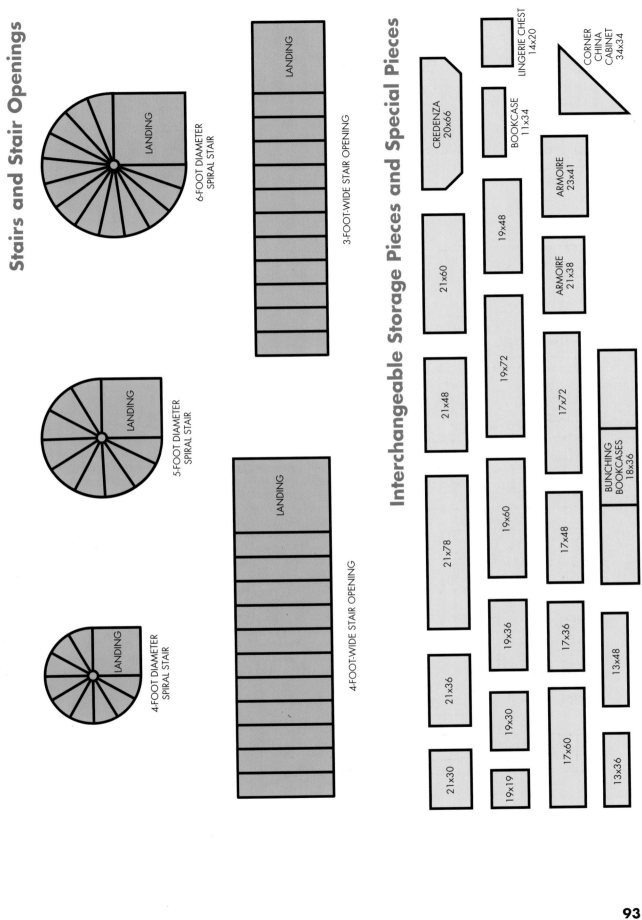

6-FOOT DIAMETER SPIRAL STAIR

LANDING

5-FOOT DIAMETER SPIRAL STAIR

LANDING

4-FOOT DIAMETER SPIRAL STAIR

LANDING

3-FOOT-WIDE STAIR OPENING

LANDING

4-FOOT-WIDE STAIR OPENING

LANDING

Interchangeable Storage Pieces and Special Pieces

CREDENZA 20x66

LINGERIE CHEST 14x20

BOOKCASE 11x34

CORNER CHINA CABINET 34x34

21x60

19x48

ARMOIRE 23x41

21x48

19x72

ARMOIRE 21x38

21x78

17x72

19x60

17x48

BUNCHING BOOKCASES 18x36

21x36

19x36

17x36

13x48

21x30

19x30

17x60

19x19

13x36

Attic Layout
Planner

Use a photocopier to reproduce this grid at its original size. Use the cutouts on pages 91–93 to help design your basement space. The scale for the grid is 1" (the dark lines) equals 1'.

What Will It Cost?

Estimating costs and establishing a budget are essential planning tools.

The final cost of your project will depend on several factors: its size, its complexity, the amount of tearout and reconstruction you need, and the quality of the materials, fixtures, and appliances that you will install. Although it's difficult for a homeowner to anticipate all expenses in advance, the best way to estimate costs is to be thoroughly familiar with your project and all its elements. That way, when you ask prospective contractors for bids (see "Working With a Contractor," pages 110–111), you'll be able to communicate effectively about changes and improvements you propose. If you request specific items such as specialty materials or products by brand name, you will make your estimates more accurate. If estimates are higher than

Mini Table of Contents

How to Use This Chapter

Your renovation may include more than one of the projects outlined in this chapter. To estimate a final cost, combine all the individual project costs. Each of the conversions are comprehensive and contain estimates for completely finishing those spaces with basic, no-frills materials. Alternatives are listed separately, but remember that all estimates are intended only as guidelines. The unique configuration of your house or additional remodeling needed for adaptations specific to your home may increase costs. Refer to the table on pages 108–109 to adjust costs for your region of the country.

what you wish to spend, your knowledge will help you discuss effective ways to lower costs by substituting less expensive materials or by eliminating portions of the project altogether. Keep the following things in mind.

■ Purchase some materials yourself. "Buying-it-yourself" is an increasingly popular aspect of home renovation and allows you to shop for bargains or to find affordable prices on luxury items. However, you will need to be very specific in discussions with your contractor about the items you will be responsible for, and you must make sure "your" materials are delivered on time.

■ Make all changes during the design phase—before you start building. Changes made during construction are usually more costly, can disrupt the work schedule, and can sometimes cause friction between you and your builder. Make sure your plan is solid, then you can go forward confidently.

■ Visit the job site often and keep lines of communication open with your builder. Often, ques-

A new shed dormer, sky windows, and built-in storage cabinets were essential in turning this unused attic space into a quiet playroom.

tions arise during construction that only the homeowner can answer. Your attentiveness will help the building process proceed smoothly.

Establishing Value

In this section are brief descriptions of popular basement remodeling projects, including pricing data from cost-estimate specialist, R.S. Means Company, Inc., Kingston, MA, a CMD Group Company. Their annual cost books and quarterly updates covering dozens of construction specialties, have been the most quoted standard for planning and estimating by the construction industry for over 57 years. For more information, contact R.S. Means at 1-800/334-3509.

Upgrading your home by converting your attic to living area will increase the value of your property and make your home more attractive to prospective buyers if you decide to sell. Each project increases home value at a different rate, however. For example, adding a bathroom is one of the most valuable improvements you can make. According to annual surveys of building contractors and real estate agents, a new bathroom can recoup more than 90 percent of the costs of construction. With an increasing number of people working in

their homes, the home office is another high-value project, recovering more than 70 percent of construction costs. As you plan, remember to not over-improve your house by making it considerably more valuable than other houses in your neighborhood. Your proposed renovation should not increase the price of your home more than 15 percent of the average price of houses in your area. That way, the cost of the upgrade will be easier to recover if and when you sell your home. If you're unsure about recovery values, consult with a real estate agent who is familiar with your area.

You probably won't undertake an attic conversion based on resale value alone. If you plan to live in your home for years, you will likely base your decisions more on increased livability and convenience than on resale value. Insist on quality materials and workmanship that will make your project a sound investment and an enjoyable space for years to come.

Full Attic

This project outlines the cost of finishing an attic space that is 16 feet wide and 36 feet long. It includes the installation of partition walls, knee walls, windows, insulation, electric baseboard heaters, new electrical outlets and lights, and all finish materials. Note that the windows supplied are large enough to comply with building code requirements in the event a room is used as a bedroom.

Also included is the cost of installing joists to create a flat ceiling along the entire length of the attic, but the estimate does not provide for additional costs for strengthening floor joists or rafters. The estimate also does not include a new stairway or modifications to an existing stairway.

The finish materials chosen are basic and readily available in most regions of the country. The walls are covered with ½-inch drywall and painted; casings and baseboard trim are plain pine and are also painted. The one luxury is a white oak hardwood strip floor laid over a plywood subfloor. The hardwood flooring accounts for nearly half of the total cost of materials. To lower costs, consider substituting a medium-grade carpet over ⅝-inch plywood, which will reduce the total estimate by about $3,000.

Cost of materials = $8,634

Total contractor's fee, including materials = $18,669

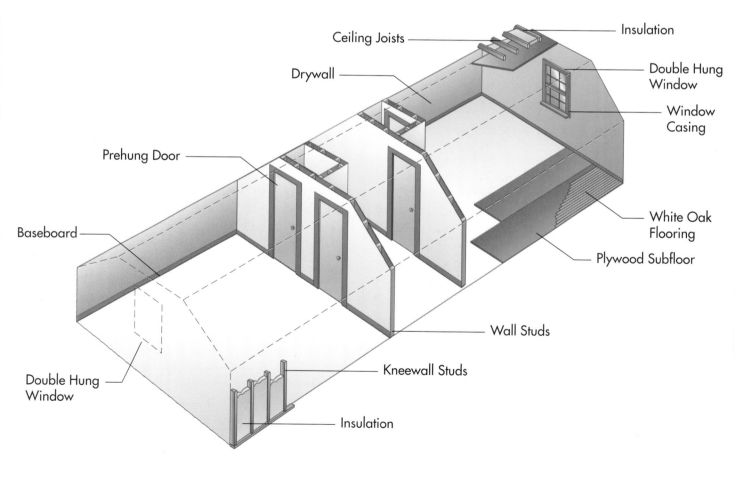

Ceiling Joists

Insulation

Double Hung Window

Drywall

Window Casing

Prehung Door

White Oak Flooring

Baseboard

Plywood Subfloor

Wall Studs

Double Hung Window

Kneewall Studs

Insulation

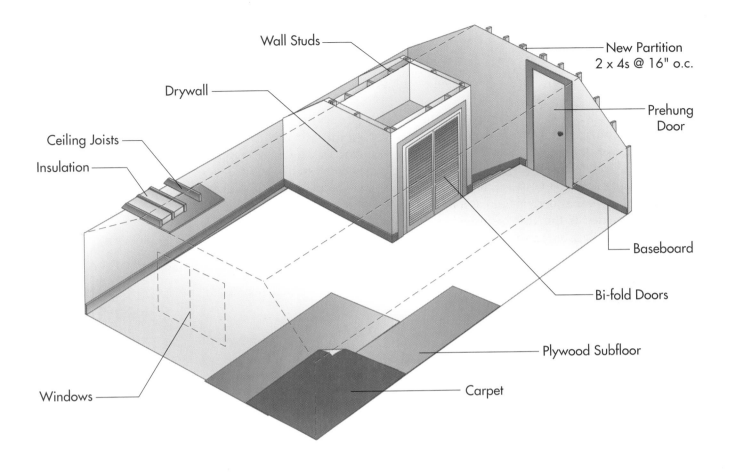

Wall Studs

Drywall

Ceiling Joists

Insulation

Windows

New Partition
2 x 4s @ 16" o.c.

Prehung
Door

Baseboard

Bi-fold Doors

Plywood Subfloor

Carpet

Half Attic

This 16x20-foot half-attic project details costs associated with finishing a portion of a typical attic space. The price includes installation of a partition wall, knee walls, a large casement window, insulation, electric baseboard heaters, new electrical outlets and lights, and all finish materials. The flooring material is a carpet installed over a ⅝-inch plywood subfloor. A passage door in the partition wall allows access to the unfinished half of the attic.

The existing peaked roofline is framed as a flat ceiling with the addition of 2x6 ceiling joists. The spaces between the joists should be filled with proper amounts of insulation—this project calls for R-19 fiberglass batts in the ceiling, but your region of the country may require a higher R-value. It is important that you vent the area above the insulation to avoid damage to framing and finish materi-

als caused by the build-up of excessive moisture. You may wish to consult with a heating and cooling specialist who can advise you about additional steps you can take to improve ventilation.

This project includes a single window large enough to meet building code requirements for emergency egress. However, if the room is to be used as a bedroom, or on a daily basis as a home office, you may wish to consider additional improvements such as an operable skylight that will encourage air circulation.

Cost of materials = $2,952

Total contractor's fee, including materials = $7,261

Gable
Dormer

The exterior of gable dormers should match the style and materials used on the exterior of your house. They also must be scaled correctly so that they are in proportion to the overall dimensions of your home. The width of this project—4 feet—is representative of the small-sized dormers that usually are grouped in twos or threes along one side of a roof.

This project uses common but durable building materials that are readily available at lumber outlets and home-improvement stores. Asphalt roofing shingles commonly come with a 30-year guarantee. The vinyl siding and the aluminum fascia and soffit should provide years of maintenance-free service. The 3x3½-foot double-hung window is clad with weather-resistant plastic. Specialized materials, such as premium wood siding or cedar shakes for the roof, will add to the overall cost.

Gable dormers are tricky to frame and require considerable carpentry skill. Working on any dormer project involves some risk, and particularly steep roofs or those more than two stories above ground may require special scaffolding. That could add to final costs. The largest portion of the labor needed, however, will be devoted to tearing off old roofing materials, removing portions of the existing roof rafters, and cutting a hole for the dormer.

Cost of materials = $732

Total contractor's fee, including materials = $2,062

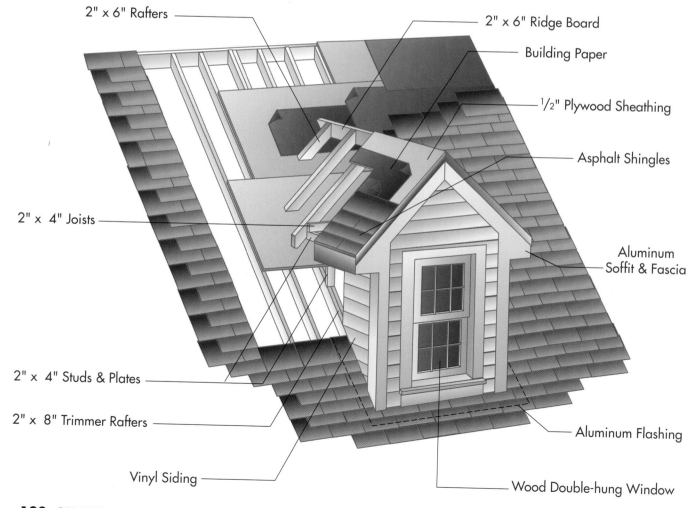

2" x 6" Rafters

2" x 6" Ridge Board

Building Paper

½" Plywood Sheathing

Asphalt Shingles

2" x 4" Joists

Aluminum Soffit & Fascia

2" x 4" Studs & Plates

2" x 8" Trimmer Rafters

Aluminum Flashing

Vinyl Siding

Wood Double-hung Window

Shed Dormer

Shed dormers are not as complex or architecturally graceful as gable dormers, but they generally provide more living area. They typically are larger structures than their gabled-dormer counterparts. Nevertheless you should scale them to fit the size of your house and finish them with similar siding and roofing materials so that they establish architectural harmony. You can allow an exception for a dormer roof pitched lower than 3 in 12. In this case, use rolled roofing that matches the color of the existing roofing instead of the asphalt shingles specified in this description.

This 12-foot-wide shed dormer features durable, maintenance-free materials including vinyl siding, fascia and soffits. The window is a double-hung, side-by-side unit that is 4x3 feet and complies with most code requirements for safety egress. A gutter is not specified for this project but may be necessary, especially if the dormer is positioned over a doorway. This example includes insulation but not the cost of finishing the interior surfaces.

Cost of materials = $1,290

Total contractor's fee, including materials = $4,459

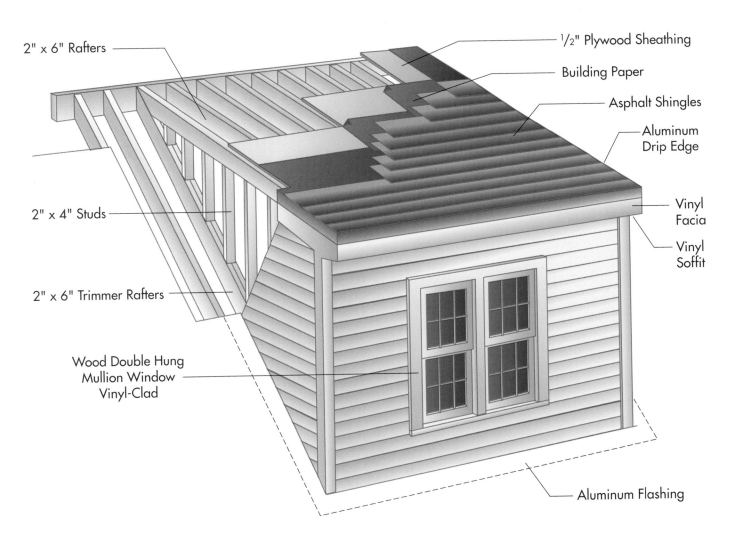

2" x 6" Rafters

2" x 4" Studs

2" x 6" Trimmer Rafters

Wood Double Hung Mullion Window Vinyl-Clad

½" Plywood Sheathing

Building Paper

Asphalt Shingles

Aluminum Drip Edge

Vinyl Facia

Vinyl Soffit

Aluminum Flashing

Stairway Renovation

This project involves the renovation of an existing 4-foot-wide stairway that rises to an unfinished attic space. The example includes the cost of tearing out the old stairway and replacing it with a new one. Note, however, that the project does not include the significant cost of alterations required for a completely new stair access. When retrofitting a house to include a new stair access, you should consult with a general contractor or knowledgeable building professional to obtain an estimate of costs.

This straight run of stairs rises a total of 8½ feet and is typical for homes with a standard ceiling height of 8 feet. The materials specified are milled specifically for use as stair parts and are chosen for their beauty and durability. Oak starting and landing newels and an oak handrail offer the warm and timeless look of wood. The oak treads and risers are particularly long-wearing and are widely available. To save costs, you can install less expensive treads and risers and cover the stairs with carpet.

Cost of materials = $1,405

Total contractor's fee, including materials = $3,661

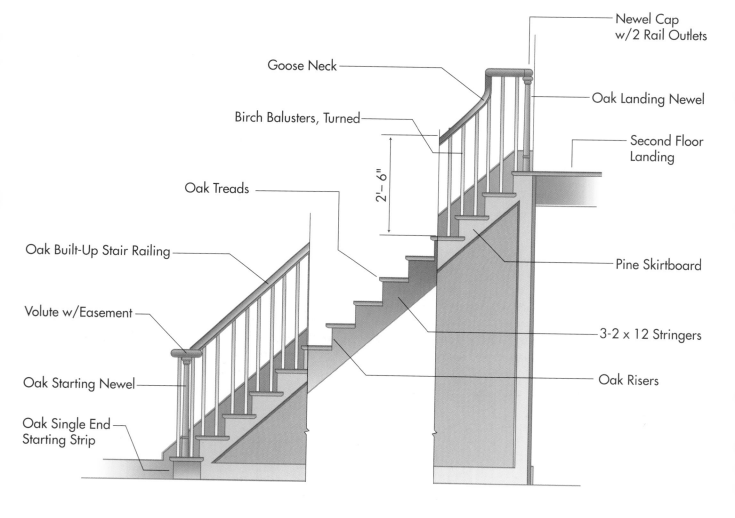

Newel Cap w/2 Rail Outlets

Goose Neck

Birch Balusters, Turned

Oak Landing Newel

Second Floor Landing

2'- 6"

Oak Treads

Oak Built-Up Stair Railing

Pine Skirtboard

Volute w/Easement

3-2 x 12 Stringers

Oak Starting Newel

Oak Risers

Oak Single End Starting Strip

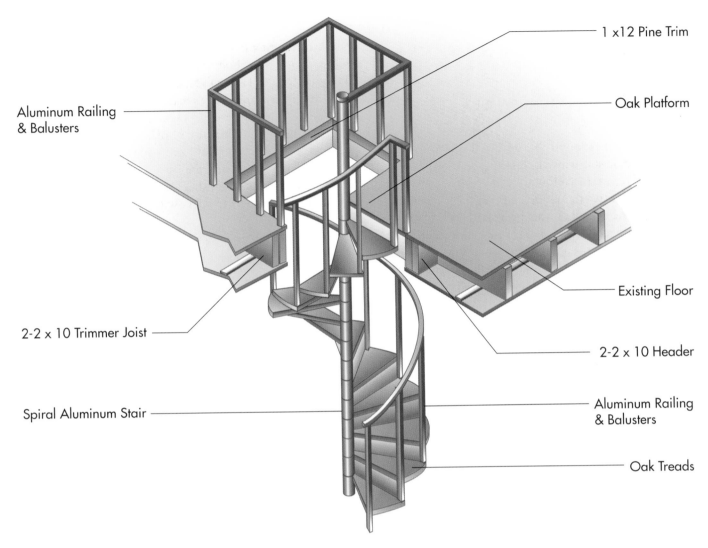

Aluminum Railing & Balusters

1 x12 Pine Trim

Oak Platform

2-2 x 10 Trimmer Joist

Existing Floor

2-2 x 10 Header

Spiral Aluminum Stair

Aluminum Railing & Balusters

Oak Treads

Spiral Stairway

When space is precious, a spiral stairway can provide access to attic rooms while taking up a minimum of floor area. This 5-foot-diameter stairway is a pre-fabricated unit featuring a heavy aluminum or steel framework with oak treads. The upper opening is protected by an aluminum railing and balusters manufactured as part of the unit.

The project costs include cutting an opening in the ceiling to gain access to the floor above, and installation of the stairway. Costs are included for for the installation of additional structural support below the stairway to adequately carry the concentrated weight of the unit.

However, if you must remove flooring or ceiling materials to install additional support, that removal as well as the subsequent floor or ceiling repair should be treated as an additional cost.

Locating a new stairway into an attic space is a primary focus of any attic conversion project. You'll need to consider carefully where the new stairway enters the attic to ensure adequate headroom. Some regions have building codes that specify minimum requirements for spiral stairways. Be sure to check local codes before proceeding.

Cost of materials = $4,074

Total contractor's fee, including materials = $6,745

Walk-in Closet

Adding storage is a typical goal of an attic conversion plan. Attic storage closets often put to good use some of the awkwardly shaped areas created by slanted ceilings—places that cannot be used for living space. A full closet allows room for hanging items, such as clothes and coats, and smaller items that fit in the shorter areas at the rear of the unit.

This project features interior walls and ceiling lined with particleboard made with aromatic cedar to deter bugs and other pests. The exterior is covered with drywall which can be finished to match any decor. Its generous 6x8-foot dimensions are sized for walk-in use, and the project includes a door, a fluorescent light fixture, and a wall-mounted light switch. You can construct this closet in either unused or finished attic areas. The trim specified here is plain and may be upgraded for additional cost.

If the closet is built to enhance an everyday living area, you should first insulate the knee wall and the rafters above the ceiling. Make sure the insulation in the rafters has at least a 1-inch gap above it to allow air circulation and prevent moisture build-up.

Cost of materials = $847

Total contractor's fee, including materials = $2,210

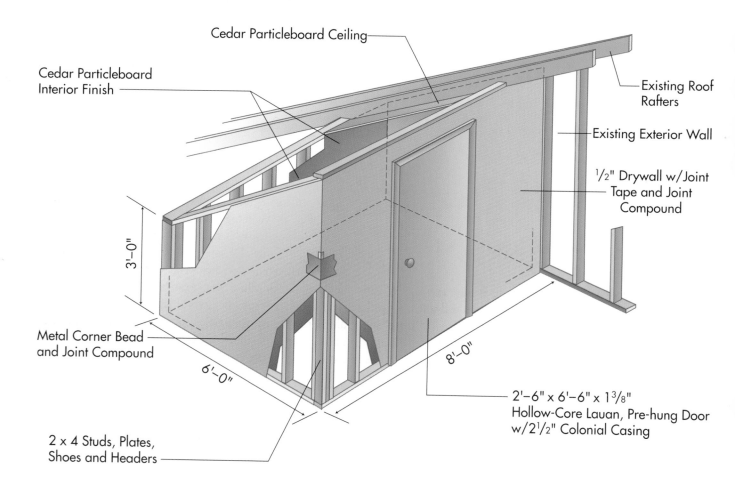

Cedar Particleboard Ceiling

Cedar Particleboard Interior Finish

Existing Roof Rafters

Existing Exterior Wall

1/2" Drywall w/Joint Tape and Joint Compound

3'-0"

Metal Corner Bead and Joint Compound

6'-0"

8'-0"

2'-6" x 6'-6" x 1 3/8" Hollow-Core Lauan, Pre-hung Door w/2 1/2" Colonial Casing

2 x 4 Studs, Plates, Shoes and Headers

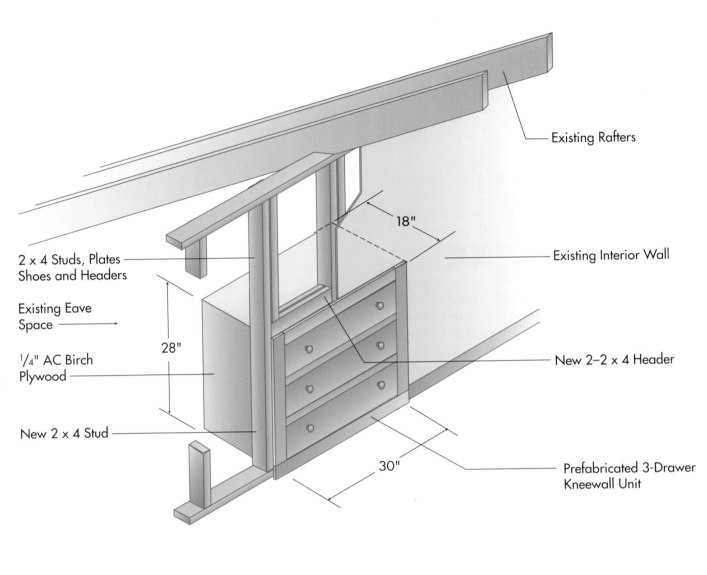

Existing Rafters

18"

Existing Interior Wall

2 x 4 Studs, Plates Shoes and Headers

Existing Eave Space

28"

1/4" AC Birch Plywood

New 2–2 x 4 Header

New 2 x 4 Stud

30"

Prefabricated 3-Drawer Kneewall Unit

Knee Wall

Knee walls help define attic living areas, but the space behind them is often neglected and unused. You can take advantage of this space by installing built-in storage units that won't take up valuable floor space or intrude into family traffic patterns. One of the most efficient designs for knee wall installations is a storage unit with pull-out drawers. Drawers allow you to easily retrieve stored items without having to resort to getting down on your hands and knees to access a cabinet recess or a fixed compartment.

This project includes framing an opening for the unit, building an enclosure of plywood, and installing a pre-fabricated storage unit with three drawers. The finished unit is 30 inches wide, 28 inches high, and 18 inches deep, and you can typically find it ready-to-install at home improvement centers. Depending on your available space, you may wish to group several similar storage units along one or more walls. If possible, install the units above the baseboard to provide an uninterrupted flow of the trim around the room.

Cost of materials = $168

Total contractor's fee, including materials = $513

Fixed Skylight

Installing a skylight is one of the best ways to bring generous amounts of light to the interiors of attic rooms. This project includes the cost of a 2x2-foot fixed bubble skylight—one of the most inexpensive units available. It has a double layer of plastic that is sealed to prevent condensation and to provide good energy efficiency. Because the unit cannot be opened, you should install it in rooms that already have windows that open to the outside air. It is also wise to consider the amount of sunlight that enters the skylight. Occasionally, direct sunlight provides large amounts of solar heat gain, and that can make a room uncomfortably warm. If this is a factor in your installation, you may be able to add adjustable shades or blinds under the skylight that will effectively control sunlight. Some skylights include shades as optional features, which, of course, will add to the cost of the unit.

As with any conversion that involves cutting a hole in the roof, you must install a skylight with exceptional care. This project calls for a wooden "curb" to be built on site and sealed against the weather. Make sure the written agreement with your contractor specifies a guarantee for workmanship and ensures that any leaks resulting from the installation will be promptly fixed free of charge.

Cost of materials = $310

Total contractor's fee, including materials = $724

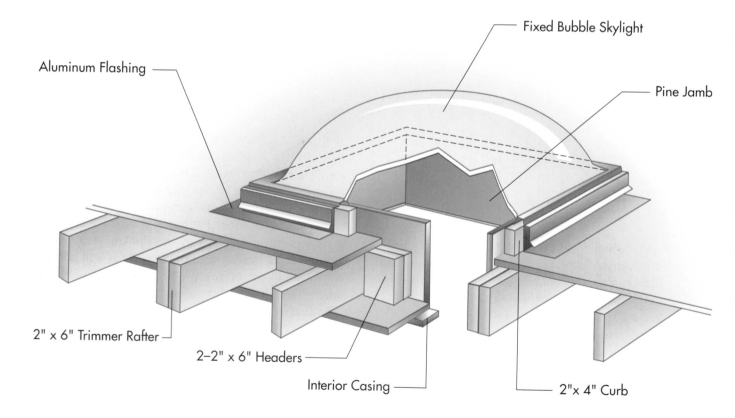

Fixed Bubble Skylight

Aluminum Flashing

Pine Jamb

2" x 6" Trimmer Rafter

2–2" x 6" Headers

Interior Casing

2" x 4" Curb

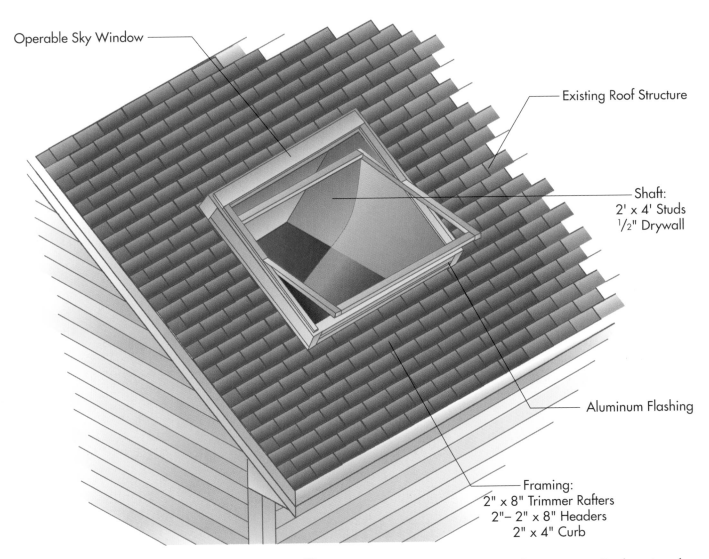

Operable Sky Window

Existing Roof Structure

Shaft:
2' x 4' Studs
1/2" Drywall

Aluminum Flashing

Framing:
2" x 8" Trimmer Rafters
2"– 2" x 8" Headers
2" x 4" Curb

Operable Sky Window

A sky window differs from a bubble skylight in that it features flat glazing and includes a variety of options that are usually associated only with premium windows. The 44x57-inch example specified here is a top-of-the-line model with glass that is tempered, insulated, and tinted for an extra measure of energy efficiency. It opens easily and tilts inward for cleaning. The price of the unit represents almost half of the total cost of the project.

If the sky window is installed at a location on the roof where there is nothing beneath it in the interior—in a section where the interior ceiling is also slanted—then you'll need only minimum materials to finish the inside window opening. Such an installation typically requires a 10- to 14-inch wood jamb covered with drywall. However, other locations—above a flat ceiling, for example—may require that you construct a shaft that extends from the window frame to the interior of the attic room, possibly for a distance of several feet. A shaft of this dimension is not a complicated undertaking, but it will add to the overall cost of the project. You may want to widen the bottom of the shaft to maximize the distribution of daylight from the sky window.

Cost of materials = $1,111

Total contractor's fee, including materials = $2,246

Standard Window

If your attic includes a gable end, you'll likely want to take advantage of it by installing a window for light and ventilation. This project includes the installation of a typical, vinyl-clad 3x4-foot double-hung window topped by a small, fixed, circle-top window for added architectural interest. The unit specified here includes insulated glass for thermal efficiency. Select your window so it's in keeping with the style of your house and the configuration of the other windows.

Standard window installation is straightforward and usually requires no significant modifications to your house. Bearing walls require you to construct

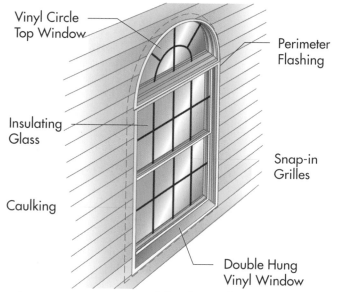

Vinyl Circle Top Window

Perimeter Flashing

Insulating Glass

Snap-in Grilles

Caulking

Double Hung Vinyl Window

temporary supports while the wall studs are cut away and replaced with the framed window opening. Creating an opening in masonry walls, such as brick or stone, will increase the cost of the overall project. An attic location that is unusually high—for example, the upper level of a three-story house—may require that you raise a temporary scaffolding at additional cost.

Cost of materials = $456

Total contractor's fee, including materials = $906

The costs described in this chapter are based on national averages for labor and materials. To adjust these figures for your location, multiply the cost shown in each project by the factor given in this table.

Alabama
Birmingham	.84
Mobile	.83
Montgomery	.82

Alaska
Anchorage	1.27
Fairbanks	1.27
Juneau	1.26

Arizona
Flagstaff	.95
Phoenix	.93
Tucson	.91

Arkansas
Little Rock	.81
Hot Springs	.71
Pine Bluff	.80

California
Bakersfield	1.11
Los Angeles	1.11
Oakland	1.16
Pasadena	1.08
Berkeley	1.29
Sacramento	1.12

Colorado
Boulder	.90
Denver	.98
Colorado Springs	.93
Durango	.89

Connecticut
Hartford	1.05
Bridgeport	1.02
New London	1.06

Delaware
Newark	.99
Wilmington	.98
Dover	.99

District of Columbia
Washington	.94

Florida
Miami	.86
Tampa Bay	.83
Tallahassee	.78

Georgia
Atlanta	.84
Columbus	.80
Dalton	.64

Hawaii
Honolulu	1.27
Hilo	1.27

Idaho
Boise	.95
Twin Falls	.82
Lewiston	1.11

Illinois

Chicago	1.12
Rockford	1.03
Peoria	1.07
Carbondale	.96

Indiana

Indianapolis	.97
South Bend	.92
Terra Haute	.95

Iowa

Des Moines	.96
Cedar Rapids	.99
Spencer	.83

Kansas

Kansas City	.95
Colby	.88
Wichita	.89

Kentucky

Lexington	.89
Bowling Green	.94
Somerset	.77

Louisiana

New Orleans	.87
Alexandria	.79
Shreveport	.81

Maine

Portland	.89
Bangor	.93
Waterville	.81

Maryland

Annapolis	.90
Salisbury	.79
Baltimore	.92

Massachusetts

Boston	1.16
Worcester	1.12
Pittsfield	1.01

Michigan

Detroit	1.06
Bay City	.95
Grand Rapids	.91

Minnesota

Minneapolis	1.14
Duluth	1.03
Bemidji	.91

Mississippi

Jackson	.83
Meridian	.78
Biloxi	.85

Missouri

St. Louis	.99
Columbia	.96
Springfield	.85

Montana

Billings	.98
Missoula	.95
Kalispell	.94

Nebraska

Omaha	.90
Grand Island	.88
Alliance	.77

Nevada

Las Vegas	1.04
Reno	.94
Elko	.93

New Hampshire

Manchester	.96
Claremont	.80
Portsmouth	.95

New Jersey

Vineland	1.11
Atlantic City	1.11
Newark	1.15

New Mexico

Albuquerque	.89
Santa Fe	.89
Roswell	.89

New York

Staten Island	1.29
Queens	1.28
Albany	.98
Syracuse	1.01
Buffalo	1.08

North Carolina

Wilmington	.75
Greensboro	.78
Raleigh	.79

North Dakota

Fargo	.79
Bismark	.81
Minot	.81

Ohio

Cleveland	1.08
Columbus	.96
Cincinnati	.98
Marion	.91

Oklahoma

Oklahoma City	.81
Tulsa	.86
Guymon	.70

Oregon

Portland	1.09
Eugene	1.06
Klamath Falls	1.06

Pennsylvania

Pittsburgh	1.05
Philadelphia	1.12
Scranton	.97
Oil City	.90

Rhode Island

Newport	1.04
Providence	1.04

South Carolina

Columbia	.74
Charleston	.76
Rock Hill	.66

South Dakota

Sioux Falls	.89
Pierre	.87
Rapid City	.86

Tennessee

Nashville	.85
Memphis	.86
Cookeville	.70

Texas

Dallas	.91
Lubbock	.80
Houston	.89
Austin	.80

Utah

Salt Lake City	.88
Provo	.89
Price	.83

Vermont

Montpelier	.84
Brattleboro	.76
Burlington	.85

Virginia

Norfolk	.85
Richmond	.85
Roanoke	.79

Washington

Seattle	1.00
Spokane	1.01
Wenatchee	.97

West Virginia

Charleston	.94
Clarksburg	.97
Martinsburg	.78

Wisconsin

Milwaukee	1.01
Madison	.97
Green Bay	.99

Wyoming

Cheyenne	.88
Casper	.88
Worland	.81

Working With A Contractor

Unless you are an accomplished do-it-yourselfer with plenty of time to devote to a project, you will probably need to hire a professional building contractor. Selecting a contractor is one of the most important aspects of getting your project done to your satisfaction. Take the time necessary to choose a contractor who has a good reputation and who is someone you feel comfortable with.

A licensed contractor is one who has completed state requirements to perform various types of work. General contractors have a broad knowledge of all aspects of construction and are hired to organize and complete a job according to an agreed-upon schedule. Other contractors, called subcontractors, have a more specific area of expertise. Electrical contractors, for example, have passed a state certification program that permits them to perform work relating to electrical hookups. It is your general contractor's responsibility to hire all subcontractors necessary to complete your project. A good general contractor has established relationships with many reliable subcontractors and can be counted on to furnish quality work that is completed in a timely fashion.

Hiring a Contractor

To find a qualified general contractor:

■ Ask friends, neighbors, colleagues, or professional acquaintances for names of reliable contractors. Make sure you have several recommendations to choose from.

■ Meet with prospective contractors to discuss your project. Ask about their experience remodeling attics and what problems they have encountered. Don't hesitate to ask for a "ballpark" figure for your particular project. A ballpark figure isn't a precise bid and you should not regard it as an agreement of any kind. Discussing money, however, will give you some idea of how knowledgeable contractors are and how comfortable they will be when it comes to talking about specific costs.

Also ask them how long they have been in business, and if they carry insurance. Without insurance, you are liable for any accidents that occur on your property. Most contractors have a certificate of insurance. It is an acceptable part of the process to request that you see the certificate before proceeding. A contractor should have insurance to cover damage, liability, and worker's compensation.

Gauge your interaction carefully. How you feel about a prospective contractor is an important factor in deciding who will get the job.

■ Obtain references from contractors and take the time to inspect their work. Reliable contractors should provide this information readily and will be proud to have their work on display. Check with your local Better Business Bureau to see if any complaints have been filed about your candidates.

■ Narrow your choices—select three to five contractors—and ask for final bids. Make sure all contractors have similar deadlines for submitting bids—about three weeks should be sufficient. Eliminate from contention any contractor who posts a late bid without a reasonable excuse; having too much work is not a valid excuse.

■ Review each bid carefully to see how thoroughly the bids have been researched. A bid should include itemized lists of materials, itemized figures for installation work, a timeline with stages of completion clearly defined, and an amount specified for the contractor's fee—usually 10 to 15 percent of the total costs. The best contractors will offer a penalty for work that is not completed in a reasonable amount of time. There also should be an agreed-upon rate for change orders. Change orders occur when you decide to make alterations to the plan or to the type of materials specified. Although most contractors will work hand-in-hand with clients to make minor changes, some alterations cause work delays that disrupt shipping arrangements or cause a contractor to alter schedules with other jobs. The best way to avoid changes is to plan thoroughly, well in advance.

■ When it comes to final selection, take all factors into account, including price. Be skeptical of any bid that seems quite a bit lower than others—the lowest bidder is not always the one who will give the most satisfying results.

■ Once you find your contractor, you should make an effort to keep lines of communication open. Schedule regular meetings to discuss progress and keep informed of interim deadlines. Tell your contractor that you don't expect to make your final payment until the job has passed all required building inspections, you have seen written proof that all subcontractors and suppliers have been paid, and you and your contractor have walked through the project and agreed that the job is complete.

Getting Bids

Creating bids for your project is not just the job of your prospective contractors—you have some responsibilities, too. Your primary responsibility will be to furnish detailed blueprint drawings and a complete materials list. Blueprints usually are produced by a registered architect, but a qualified designer or even the homeowner can create usable plans. Blueprints from a registered architect can be given directly to a contractor for bids, but plans produced by a designer or the homeowner must first be reviewed, approved, and stamped by a registered structural engineer.

The materials list should be as complete and comprehensive as possible. It should specify the quantity and brand names of materials needed, and the brand names and model numbers of fixtures and appliances that are to be installed. If specific companies are not identified, then the contractor will furnish brands he or she is familiar with.

Many homeowners enjoy being involved in the selection process and like to shop for specialty items themselves. Be sure your contractor understands your intentions and the materials list indicates any purchases you intend to make. Both you and your contractor must agree about any possible limitations due to size, weight, and other relevant factors.

When bids start to arrive, study them to see how each was prepared and the level of detail each contractor provides. A meticulously prepared bid usually indicates that the contractor has given careful consideration to your project and is prepared for potential problems. If all the bids vary widely, you should review each bid with the contractor who prepared it to discover reasons why. It may be that certain items or tasks have been omitted. Make sure all the prospective contractors are working with

identical information about your plans. A contractor may be willing to resubmit another bid based on new criteria or information.

Making a Contract

Once you have made your selection, you should sign a written contract with your contractor. Many contractors have prepared contract forms. If you are unsure about the specific points of a contract, you should consult with an attorney before proceeding to sign any document.

Contracts are not all alike, but a good contract should cover the following points:

■ A precise description of all work to be completed by the contractor and subcontractors, and a description of all materials that are to be installed.

■ The total cost of the job, including all materials, labor, and fees.

■ A schedule of payments that you will make to the contractor. Be wary of contracts asking for large up-front payments—some states even limit the amount of up-front payments made to contractors before work begins.

■ A work schedule with calendar dates specified for the completion of each stage of the project. The schedule should include an allowance for delays due to delivery problems, weather-related interruptions, and back orders of scarce products.

■ A "right of recision" that allows the homeowner to back out of the contract within 72 hours of signing.

■ A certificate of insurance that guarantees the contractor has the appropriate insurance.

■ A warranty that guarantees that the labor and materials are free from defects for a certain period of time, usually one year.

■ An arbitration clause that specifies a method that you and your contractor will use to settle any disputes about materials, quality, or charges.

■ A description of change-order procedures stating what will happen if you decide to make alterations to the plans or specifications after the contract has been signed. The description should include a fee structure for change requests.

■ A release of liens that assures homeowners they won't incur liens or charges against their property as a result of legal actions filed against the contractor or any of the subcontractors.

Index

Numbers in **bold** indicate pages with photographs.